PERINI RANCH

EST · 1983

RANCH

STEAKHOUSE
COOKBOOK

PERINI

EST **RANCH** 1983

STEAKHOUSE

COOKBOOK

LISA AND **TOM PERINI**

WITH **CHERYL ALTERS JAMISON**
PHOTOGRAPHS BY **WYATT McSPADDEN**

CIDER MILL PRESS

BOOK
PUBLISHERS

CONTENTS

Introduction

A CELEBRATION OF HISTORY, HERITAGE, AND HOME ON THE RANCH

As we look back on more than 40 years of the Perini Ranch Steakhouse, a word that comes up time and time again is celebration. The two of us are incredibly fortunate to be part of a place that makes people happy. Somewhat through intention and somewhat through sheer luck, we have created a one-of-a-kind setting where people smile as they walk through our screen door. Customers have to put in some effort to get to our rural corner of West Texas. It's not easy to find Perini Ranch. It's not on a main highway or major thoroughfare, and people tell us that our signage leaves a little to be desired (there isn't any). When they finally pull up to this old ranch barn sitting in the midst of a live oak grove, they find that we're all weathered wood, concrete floors, corrugated tin, and mismatched tables and chairs. The overall effect is greater than the sum of its parts, because it seems to make folks feel right at home. Customers arrive here from around the world, and mark birthdays, anniversaries, and just the fact that they made it through another week. That makes us feel very grateful, as well as celebratory. We hope you'll feel special too, reading and cooking from this book.

WE'RE NOT JUST DINNER, WE'RE A DESTINATION

These days, the spokes that keep our wagon wheel turning, as we like to say, involve not just the Steakhouse on the Perini Ranch but—in the heart of nearby Buffalo Gap—the Gap Café, a Western saloon–style space for special events and programming, and a Supper Club for special events, and the Country Market for all manner of tableware, signature foods, and items for the kitchen and home. We offer lodging in our Guest Quarters, two renovated classic Texas homes with ranch views that stretch forever. The Main House is an 1885-era farmhouse original to the property that can sleep five. The Camp House sleeps three. We have a full catering and special events staff that arranges events from coast-to-coast, along with a robust mail-order business. Dinner at the Steakhouse, though, certainly remains at the heart of our operation.

Our menu revolves around beef, recognized as the food for celebration. No one gets a raise or an award and hears "You've done a hell of a job. I'm going to take you out for a chicken breast!" Nope. You go out for a great steak. We have always focused on serving high-quality beef, most of it Certified Angus Beef cooked over mesquite coals—grilled ribeyes, sizzling fajitas, smoked prime rib, barbecued brisket, chicken-fried steak, and the quintessential cheeseburger. Rustic wood-fire-cooked food delights people. Most of our preparations are simple, good, and celebratory, and have a South by Southwest, or Southwest by South,

inspiration. Initially the Steakhouse served just a handful of comforting side dishes. They weren't fancy, but in an era of fast-food French fries, our homey green chile hominy, zucchini Perini, greens with potlikker, and skillet-cooked cowboy potatoes made people sit up and take notice. We are both a little amused and confused by the farm-to-table "movement." To us, that's business as usual. We've always called it gardening.

Our first few desserts were the homey type too, things grandmothers used to whip up routinely back when rural life was at its height. We're thinking of dishes like freshly baked shortcake with strawberries plucked from the garden that morning, accompanied by heavy cream from down the road. Dishes like that had nearly died out by the time we started. Bread pudding with whiskey sauce is all over menus today, but we were among the only places serving it regularly back in the day. We've added quite a few recipes to our repertoire over the years and are pleased to share many of them with you on these pages. We hope you'll enjoy them, whether made in your home or during a visit to Perini Ranch.

WE'RE SO GLAD YOU'RE HERE

Another reason people feel celebratory when they come to the ranch is because our staff makes them feel welcome. What a crew we have! Front of the house, back of the house, ranch hands—they all understand that Texas hospitality is our business. We put a lot of effort into training everyone, but that wouldn't be worth much if they weren't warm, caring people to start. Some of these great folks have been with us for decades. The two of us love hosting our guests too. As a child, Tom was a bad student because of then-undiagnosed dyslexia. The upside was that he put a lot of effort into developing an outgoing

personality. That characteristic has served him well, especially as founder, visionary, and official host of the Steakhouse.

The ranch is home to some gregarious four-legged mascots too. You might glimpse our trio of long and low Bassett hounds—Jett, Winston, and Oliver—who ride all over the ranch, ears flapping. We also tend a small herd of longhorns, with horn spreads much wider than we are tall. Some folks think those are our beef cattle. Heck no, that would make some tough eating. They're pets, all with names.

IT'S WHAT IT IS, BECAUSE OF WHERE IT IS

We are a country joint on a small family ranch in a town off the beaten path. The most popular tee-shirt that we sell asks: "Where the Hell is Buffalo Gap?" The town and ranch are nestled at the northwestern edge of the Texas Hill Country, where it meets the high plains of the Llano Estacado, about a dozen miles south of Abilene. For a brief period in the late 19th century, Buffalo Gap was the county seat of Taylor County and a happening place. Through some political maneuvering, the county seat was transferred to Abilene, by then a booming rail-

road town, leaving Buffalo Gap to never grow beyond a town whose residents only number in the hundreds. Bison did used to thunder through the area, between two mesas that define the landscape here, giving Buffalo Gap its name. It's remarkable, beautiful land, and we're privileged to reside in such a spot.

It took a while for customers to discover the Steakhouse. We had supporters from nearby ranches, the town, and Abilene, the closest city, from day one, but it took a good dozen years for the Steakhouse operation to mature.

A BITE OF HISTORY, FROM TOM'S PERSPECTIVE

My parents bought this ranch back in the 1950s when the family lived in Abilene. My father, a geologist, enjoyed being a weekend rancher. Among the three Perini sons, I in particular found it a joyous place to spend time. Back then, you could drive at age 14, and from that moment on, I started inviting my friends to hang out here. We might have cut school a few times. I used a beaten-up grill to cook burgers to go with the beer and liquor we managed to smuggle when our parents weren't watching. By the time I was in my 20s though, I was enjoying city life in Dallas

and selling real estate, and the ranch was far from my mind.

When Dad passed away in 1965, my mother said, "It's time to come home and manage the ranch." I wasn't thrilled with her pronouncement, but I respected my mother greatly, and didn't want this piece of family history to slip away, so back to the ranch I went. I quickly discovered that while ranching and agriculture make a wonderful lifestyle, they are difficult ways to make a living. I loved being a cowboy, but it was awfully hard work. I was fortunate to fall in with some older, more experienced ranchers—including a dear friend of my father's, Watt Matthews, from the Lambshead Ranch near Albany, Texas—who tried their best to help me out. However, between market prices, weather, insects, and other acts of God, it was a struggle to make ends meet. Heck, the ends weren't really meeting at all. I was leasing more land to make a bigger cattle operation, but seemed to make only enough money to pay taxes, then had to ask the bank to give me another loan to keep it going.

I found myself remembering the simpler times when I went to the ranch and grilled those burgers, and found myself wanting to spend time cooking rather than cowboy-ing. I've always been fascinated with Texas history and was drawn further to cooking through the old chuck wagon tradition of feeding the cowboys and ranch hands. I had seen a lot of the old wagons around the ranches of the area, but these mobile kitchens were falling into disrepair, a relic from an earlier time, when the range was open and epic cattle drives were the way to get cattle to market. So I got a chuck wagon and started cooking up the cowboy classics—beans, biscuits, briskets, and more—in Dutch ovens and over live fires. I learned by doing, with those cowboys being some tough critics, but I did learn.

I was still ranching as word got around that I was a pretty decent cowboy cook. I was invited to bring the chuck wagon to an increasing number of events—cattle or horse sales, family reunions, weddings. I didn't realize it yet, but I had become a caterer. The size of the parties grew and grew to hundreds. The food wasn't fancy, but it was good Texas food. The money I made went back to support the cattle operation. Cattle prices were tanking and the business of running cattle was looking as profitable as the beer concession at a Baptist picnic.

Watt Matthews, dad's friend and by now a real mentor to me, had been observing all of this. He made a pronouncement just as pivotal to my life as Mother's had been about returning to the ranch years earlier. "Tom, you need to sell out. You can do more for the beef industry by cooking beef than raising it." Because the idea came from such a respected source, in 1983 I decided to give it a try. After selling off the cattle operation, I converted an old hay barn into the Perini Ranch Steakhouse. At first, the restaurant didn't even have a sign, and the opening menu was written on a Big Chief paper tablet. We served mostly barbecue, but people kept asking for steaks. I had grown up knowing the traditions of great West Texas steakhouses, places like Lowake Steak

House in Rowena, and Zentner's, that had locations in San Angelo and Abilene, so I had some idea of what they might want. We grilled them all over fragrant mesquite, our native wood.

Those early years were tough and lean. I remember Mother loaning me enough money to make payroll. It was truly just a loan; she tracked every cent of it. In 1995, the business began to turn around. I credit that to four things: I was invited by the James Beard Foundation to cook at the James Beard House in New York. Cooking at the Beard House is considered the culinary equivalent of a musician playing Carnegie Hall. While being a great honor, it was also a great expense. I decided I might be able to rationalize the cost by getting a little New York–based publicity. Before the trip I shipped Mesquite Smoked Peppered Beef Tenderloins to key media. They weren't even on our regular menu, but I was cooking them up for events, and knew they were special. You'll find the whole story of this adventure on page 75, but the tenderloin ended up being selected by the *New York Times* as the year's best mail-order holiday gift. That was followed by Governor George W. Bush asking me to cater a tailgate party at the Texas Governor's Mansion in Austin for a University of Texas football game. I was in high cotton. If those events weren't momentous enough, I also met Lisa, who was willing to marry me and my restaurant. As a bonus, she brought experience in the marketing, retail, and restaurant industries. She gradually took over the role of operations manager for the business and was instrumental in growing it into what we have today.

CELEBRATING THE PROUD HERITAGE OF TEXAS RANCHING

We consider it key to our mission to help preserve Texas history by celebrating our ranching and agricultural roots, as well as those folks who carry it on. Historically, the Lone Star State has been defined by its ranches, majestic spreads stretching for vast numbers of miles. They measure in the hundreds of thousands of acres, sometimes larger than the state of Rhode

Island. Some like the XIT, King Ranch, and Four Sixes developed mythic reputations. *Giant*, perhaps the most iconic film ever made in, and about, Texas, featured a ranch called Reata that almost stole the show from Elizabeth Taylor, James Dean, and Rock Hudson.

This legacy dates to the post–Civil War period. Men had returned home from the war needing to make a living, and discovered that the millions of wild cattle scattered across Texas could be rounded up and driven to market. It was extremely difficult work, but began building wealth as well as an epic heritage. Author Larry McMurtry immortalized the cattle drive in his Pulitzer Prize–winning *Lonesome Dove*, and our friend actor Robert Duvall helped another generation appreciate the era, starring in the 1985 Emmy Award–winning miniseries adapted from the book. His larger-than-life character, Augustus McCrae, even provided the name of our first Bassett hound, Gus.

To help us explore and celebrate the cattle and beef business back to those mid-19th-century beginnings, we were honored to host a series of podcasts called "Meet Me at the Wagon," with *Texas Monthly* magazine as a part of our 40th anniversary year in 2023. Guests who gave their insights included cowboy entertainer Red Steagall, chefs Stephan Pyles and Dean Fearing, ranchers Jon Means and John Dudley, former Governor Rick Perry, and meat scientist Dr. Jeff Savell, who is the vice chancellor and dean for Agriculture and Life Sciences at Texas A&M University. The podcasts continue to live online, if you want to hear more about this storied history.

HOME ON THE RANCH

Circling back to our own Perini Ranch and businesses, Tom's need to sell off the cattle operation ultimately has created more cause for celebration. We are thankful to have been able to stay on Tom's family's land, because truly, family is at the center of it all. Tom's mother understood that many years ago. The two of us have gotten to work together for decades, nurturing the various parts of businesses like they were children. And speaking of children, Tom's daughters, Caroline and Jessica, both helped out at the Steakhouse in their younger years. Caroline even went into the restaurant business in Dallas, and is in the process of opening her own hospitality project in the heart of Buffalo Gap. We know the Perini legacy will continue for years ahead. It is our great pleasure and honor to share all of this with you, in person and through this cookbook. We hope you'll enjoy the ride—and the recipes—as much as we have. We look forward to celebrating with you soon!

COWBOY BREAKFASTS

Good morning! You've always heard that breakfast is the most important meal of the day. Well, we're not sure about that, but we think it's a good idea to begin your day with a bountiful ranch breakfast. We added The Gap Café to our stable of businesses a few years ago to offer many of these dishes, along with the kind of strong black coffee cowboys have always favored. It's just down the road from our ranch in the heart of Buffalo Gap. Stop by if you're in the neighborhood.

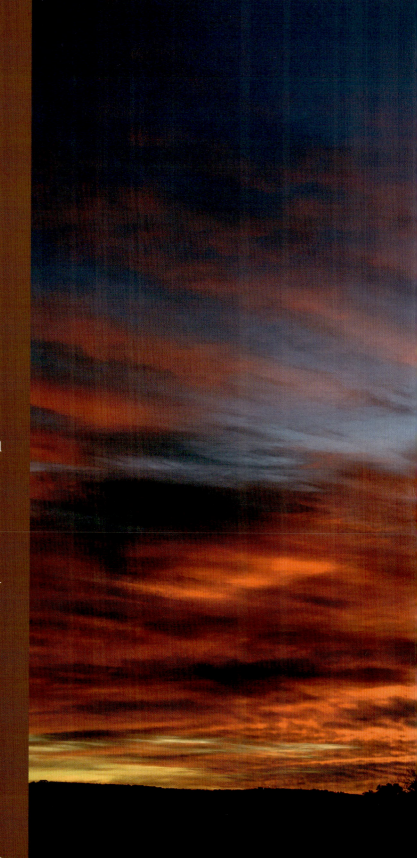

Biscuits and Sausage Gravy

SERVES 4 TO 6

BISCUITS

2 cups all-purpose flour, plus more for rolling out dough

2 teaspoons baking powder

½ teaspoon baking soda

¾ teaspoon table salt

¼ cup (½ stick) cold salted butter, cubed

1 cup buttermilk

SAUSAGE GRAVY

1 pound bulk breakfast sausage

3 tablespoons all-purpose flour

2 cups whole milk

2 teaspoons freshly cracked black pepper, or more to taste

1 teaspoon table salt, or more to taste

Pinch of cayenne, optional

Biscuits have been a ranch staple for as long as there have been ranches. In the early days, and especially on cattle drives—when moving herds from South Texas to the closest railhead in Abilene, Kansas—biscuits were a part of breakfast and every other meal. The chuck wagon cook would carry sourdough starter in the wagon, guarding the living yeast with as much care as the cowboys gave their horses. Using the starter, and by adding just flour and water, cooks could create a biscuit called hard tack, really a pretty descriptive name. When quick leavenings like baking powder and baking soda became widely available, the lighter style of biscuit featured here became the norm. Tender and flaky, the biscuits are a dream on their own, or with peach preserves, but served up with sausage gravy, they become the iconic rib-sticking morning meal.

1. To Make the Biscuits: Heat the oven to 450°F. Whisk together the flour, baking powder, baking soda, and salt in a large shallow bowl. Add the cold butter and use your fingers or a pastry blender to cut it into the flour mixture, making small pea-size pieces. Add the buttermilk. With a minimum of handling, mix into a smooth dough.

Put the dough on a lightly floured work surface. With a rolling pin, roll out to a generous ½-inch thickness. Using a floured 2½- to 3-inch biscuit cutter, cut the dough into rounds, as close together as possible to avoid having to reroll the dough. Between cutting out the biscuits, dip the cutter into some flour so the dough doesn't stick. Lightly pat together any remaining dough scraps, reroll gently, and cut into additional rounds.

Arrange the biscuits, barely touching, on a baking sheet. Bake until risen and golden brown, about 10 minutes.

2. To Make the Gravy: While the biscuits are baking, crumble the sausage into a large heavy skillet and cook over medium heat until well browned, 5 to 8 minutes. Remove the sausage with a slotted spoon and drain on paper towels. Stir the flour into the pan drippings. Cook for a couple of minutes, to lose the raw taste of the flour. Pour in the milk, then add the pepper, salt, and if you wish, cayenne. Stir continually, until the gravy thickens enough to coat the back of a spoon. Stir the sausage back into the gravy, and heat through.

3. Split hot biscuits and arrange on plates. Spoon gravy over each and serve piping hot.

**BISCUITS AND
SAUSAGE GRAVY**

SEE PAGE 20

Breakfast Sandwiches with Spicy Mayo

MAKES 4 SANDWICHES

SPICY MAYO

¾ cup mayonnaise

1 tablespoon sriracha hot sauce

7 tablespoons unsalted butter, at room temperature, plus more for the pan

4 breakfast sausage patties, each about 3 inches across

4 slices American cheese, at room temperature

½ medium onion, thinly sliced

4 split biscuits or English muffins, or 8 slices white bread

4 large eggs

Salt and freshly ground black pepper

Breakfast sandwiches are a perfect use of biscuits like those in the previous recipe. However, if you're trying to get out the door on a busy day, toasted English muffins or slices of white bread make a good base for this morning meal. A multigrain or sourdough bread or even a croissant can be the canvas for a breakfast sandwich creation too. In summer, a thick juicy tomato slice adds to the enjoyment. The spicy mayo makes this sandwich sing!

1. Make the spicy mayo, stirring together the mayonnaise and sriracha in a small bowl.

2. Warm 2 tablespoons of the butter in a medium skillet over medium-low heat. Add the sausage patties and fry them until richly browned on one side, 6 to 7 minutes. Flip over, immediately top each with a cheese slice, and fry until the sausage is well browned, another 6 to 7 minutes. The cheese should be starting to melt too. Remove the patties to a plate and loosely cover with foil to keep warm.

3. Add the onion to the butter and sausage drippings, and sauté until the slices are beginning to brown and crisp in a few spots, 8 to 10 minutes. Scrape the onion onto the plate with the sausage and re-cover it.

4. Generously smear both sides of each biscuit, English muffin, or bread slice with 3 tablespoons of the butter. Cook in the skillet in the drippings until lightly brown and crisp on both sides, 5 to 8 minutes total. Keep the toasted bread warm.

5. Crack each egg into a cup or saucer. Melt the remaining 2 tablespoons of butter in the skillet over medium heat. Nudge the eggs one by one into the skillet, side by side. Do this in 2 batches with a bit more butter, if needed. Cook the eggs for about 1 minute, sprinkling them with salt and pepper while they fry. Gently turn the eggs, puncturing the yolks so they run a bit as they finish cooking "over hard," another 1 to 2 minutes.

6. Quickly arrange the biscuits or other bread on each of 4 plates. Smear with spicy mayo. Divide the onion mixture among them, then top each with a cheese-covered sausage patty and an egg. Assemble the sandwiches and serve immediately.

TOM'S TIP: Breakfast doesn't have to be just for breakfast. This sandwich with sausage and eggs makes a fine lunch or evening meal. Our French-Fried French Toast (page 42), for example, was created initially for a late-night supper. Lisa grew up in South Carolina, so she thinks of grits as great supper comfort food. Keep in mind too that the reverse can be true. "Dinner" dishes like grilled steaks and cowboy potatoes, served up later in this book, make themselves right at home as a part of the morning meal spread.

COFFEE AND OTHER REAL TEXAS INGREDIENTS, TWO WAYS

Perini Ranch Steakhouse food is pretty traditional, very home-style. We have some fun with our chef friends who serve much fancier dishes than we do. Legendary Texas chef Stephan Pyles, known for his flights of imaginative fancy with Texas foods, has been a buddy of ours for decades. He even grew up in Big Spring, about 90 miles down the road from our ranch. We rib each other continually about what the other serves. One time, for a conference presentation, we decided to turn these hijinks into a real show. Together we picked five iconic Texas ingredients—beef, corn, bacon, jalapeños and other chiles, and coffee—and demonstrated the difference in how we might each prepare such foods. For the coffee portion of the program, Stephan hustled around making a coffee-rubbed beef tenderloin that was then cooked sous vide. Tom sat on the other side of the stage, leisurely enjoying a fine cup of plain old black coffee. People are still talking about the hilarious results.

Breakfast Burritos

SERVES 4

2 tablespoons vegetable oil

2 tablespoons beef tallow, bacon drippings, or unsalted butter

1 large (about 12 ounces) baking potato, or 2 to 3 red or Yukon Gold potatoes, peeled or unpeeled, shredded on the large holes of a box grater or in a food processor

½ teaspoon kosher salt

Freshly ground black pepper

1 medium onion, chopped

4 large eggs, lightly beaten

4 large thin flour tortillas, warmed

8 slices crisp cooked bacon

About 1 cup grated mild Cheddar or Monterey Jack cheese, at room temperature

1 cup Moose on the Loose Salsa or other tomato and jalapeño–based salsa, or more to taste

Fresh cilantro sprigs, for garnish

Morning tacos and burritos are about as common around here these days as biscuits and gravy. A breakfast burrito can be stuffed with any number of ingredients, most commonly scrambled eggs, bacon, and potatoes. We wrap our burritos in flour tortillas made locally, daily. Linda and Paul Curtis, a couple of members of our Perini Ranch team, created the bottled Moose on the Loose Salsa included here. Canadian transplant Paul, a former Montreal Canadiens NHL hockey player, is the "moose" who found his way to Buffalo Gap. He used to make the salsa just for our crew and a few lucky friends, but now we sell it at our café and the Perini Ranch Country Market.

1. Warm the oil and tallow in a large, heavy skillet over medium heat. Stir in the potatoes, salt, and as much pepper as you wish. Pat the mixture down evenly and cook several minutes. Scrape it up from the bottom of the skillet, add the onion, and pat back down again. Repeat the process until the potatoes are cooked through and golden brown, about 12 to 15 minutes. Pour the eggs over the potatoes and scrape the mixture up and down another couple of times to distribute and cook the eggs.

2. Spoon one-quarter of the potatoes onto each tortilla. Top each with 2 slices of bacon and one-quarter of the cheese. Roll up each into a loose cylinder and plate, seam side down. We put the salsa in a little dish on the side, but you can spoon it over the burritos, if you prefer. Garnish with cilantro sprigs and serve.

TOM'S TIP: We often use leftover Cowboy Potatoes (page 221) in our burritos at home. You can vary the flavor by varying the cooking fat too. We have lots of beef tallow—rendered beef fat—which is mild but distinctive, and an excellent choice for high-heat sautéing and deep-frying. It's also considered a healthier option than highly processed vegetable oils.

Jalapeño Popper Quiche

CRUST [MAKES 2]

2⅔ cups all-purpose flour

1½ tablespoons granulated sugar

1¼ teaspoons table salt

1 cup (2 sticks) unsalted butter, cut into 12 pieces

½ cup ice water

1 large egg, beaten with 1 tablespoon water

FILLING

3 large eggs

1 large egg yolk

½ cup heavy whipping cream

¼ cup whole milk

¼ cup sour cream

1 teaspoon table salt

1 teaspoon freshly ground black pepper

4 ounces (about 1 cup) grated Gruyère cheese

2 to 4 jalapeños, seared in a skillet until blistered in a few spots, seeded, and chopped

4 slices bacon, cooked crisp and crumbled

The most popular dinner appetizer at the Steakhouse is our Jalapeño Bites (page 51). Our cream cheese–stuffed jalapeños are wrapped in bacon, then baked to a crisp, a variation on the jalapeño popper theme, where the peppers are often batter dipped and deep-fried. Here we take the combination of tastes and textures a slightly different direction, baking them up in a pie crust. We always make a second pie crust because it's no harder than a solo one, and it gives us a head start on the next meal.

1. Heat the oven to 325°F. Butter a 9-inch pie dish.

2. **To Make the Crust:** Combine the flour, sugar, and salt in a food processor. Scatter the butter over the dry ingredients and pulse until the butter is mixed in lightly and most of the pieces are about the size of peas. Add the ice water, half at a time, pulsing again, just enough to form a rough dough. Don't overmix. Scrape the dough out onto a floured board and knead a few times. Our baker and café manager, Celeste Lopez, says to knead it just until it "becomes plush like a pillow." Divide in 2 and wrap each in plastic. Freeze one for later use. Refrigerate the other half of the dough for 20 to 30 minutes.

Roll the dough out on a floured work surface, into a 10-inch round. Transfer the dough to the prepared pie dish. Crimp the edges with your thumb and fingers. Bake the crust 20 minutes, then brush the crust with the egg wash mixture. (You won't need all of it.) Continue baking until golden and lightly crisp, about 10 more minutes. Leave the oven on. Let the crust cool.

3. **To Make the Filling:** In a medium bowl, whisk together the eggs, egg yolk, cream, milk, sour cream, salt, and pepper. Scatter the cheese evenly in the pie crust, followed by the jalapeño pieces and the bacon. Pour the egg mixture over everything. Bake 25 to 30 minutes, until lightly set. If the edge of the crust is browning too much, cover it with aluminum foil. Let the quiche cool fully before slicing and serving.

BREAKFAST BURRITOS

SEE PAGE 26

Green Chile Egg and Cheese Casserole

SERVES 6 TO 8

1 cup grated pepper jack cheese

1 cup grated medium Cheddar cheese

1 cup chopped roasted mild to medium New Mexico green chiles, with any accumulated liquid, fresh or thawed if frozen

6 large eggs, separated

One 5-ounce can evaporated milk

1 tablespoon all-purpose flour

½ teaspoon kosher salt

¼ teaspoon freshly ground black pepper

Vegetable oil spray

1 medium tomato, sliced thinly

Given the choice, we almost always choose a savory breakfast over sweet. Here's a souffle-esque dish, but much more forgiving than the French classic version. With its piquant chile flavoring, the casserole is also much sassier than a French souffle. We always use the long green chile pods from neighboring New Mexico, but you could use poblanos, with their similar level of heat.

1. Heat the oven to 325°F. Butter or grease a 9x13-inch baking dish. Combine the cheeses and scatter evenly in the bottom of the dish. Pour the green chiles over the cheese and stir together. In a large bowl, mix the egg yolks with the evaporated milk, flour, salt, and pepper. Beat the egg whites in an electric mixer on high speed until stiff peaks form. Fold the egg whites into the egg yolk mixture. Spread it evenly over the chile-cheese mixture.

2. Mist a piece of foil large enough to cover the dish with vegetable oil spray. Cover the casserole with the foil and plan for a total baking time of about 65 minutes. Bake the casserole for 30 minutes. Uncover and arrange the tomato slices over the casserole. Cover it again and continue baking for about 30 minutes more, until lightly set. Uncover and bake for about 5 more minutes, until lightly colored and no longer jiggly. Scoop out portions of the casserole neatly and serve right away.

ARBUCKLES, *THE* COWBOY COFFEE OF OLD

Brothers John and Charles Arbuckle founded Arbuckles' Coffee in the post–Civil War era of the 19th century, and quickly gained a following among cowboys of the Old West. The Arbuckles developed the concept of roasting the beans for consistency, glazing them to seal in their flavor and prolong freshness, and then packaging the beans. The glaze included a touch of sweetener to further enhance the flavor. Arbuckles' Ariosa Blend was so popular that many cowboys thought of it as synonymous with the beverage. The bags held a tiny peppermint candy too, which worked as an incentive for the cowboys to help grind the coffee, since it was a rare treat. It may not sound like much these days, but during a two-month cattle drive, it was heaven in a cup. Old crates branded with the Arbuckles label are still in demand today. For your own cowboy-style brew, we package and sell Perini Ranch Cowboy Coffee, the medium-roast blend we've served at the Steakhouse since its 1983 opening. It's available as whole or ground beans at periniranch.com.

THE CHUCK WAGON: A FOOD TRUCK OF AN EARLIER AGE

From the mid-19th to somewhere in the 20th century, the chuck wagon was the ranch's rolling commissary, basically a food truck of another age. Chuck wagons served a vital role during cattle roundups and trail drives, which could take up to 2 months to get to market. Charles Goodnight, a founder and partner in the JA Ranch, built the first of these in 1866, converting a surplus Army wagon into a mobile kitchen. He outfitted it with a pantry box and a hinged door that could open to serve as a table. The wagon stored Dutch ovens, other kettles and pots, along with crossbars and hooks for holding them over a fire. There was always a large coffee pot too. Strong black coffee would accompany all meals prepared daily by the cook. The wagon would be stocked with "keepers" like dried beans and rice, flour, onions, potatoes, lard or beef tallow, spices, and condiments. The cook always kept a sourdough starter for bread and biscuits, something we talk about at length in our Biscuits & Breads chapter. The wagon also held first aid supplies, firewood, water, and various tools. The chuck wagon became nearly as iconic as the cowboys themselves.

Cowboy Hash Browns

SERVES 4 AS A MAIN DISH, OR UP TO 6 AS A SIDE DISH

2¼ to 2½ pounds red or Yukon Gold potatoes, cooked and cooled

¼ cup plus 2 tablespoons beef tallow, bacon fat, or unsalted butter

1 teaspoon table salt

1 teaspoon garlic powder

½ teaspoon freshly ground black pepper

We use red potatoes for our chunky hash browns. At The Gap Café, we deep-fry them twice, just like the way we make our French fries. For home cooks, it's simpler to start with cooked potatoes and then pan-fry them. In our personal kitchen, we've found leftovers from our Cowboy Potatoes (page 221) to be perfect. If you don't have them on hand though, simply boil up some potatoes the night before or even a few minutes before you want to make the dish. Any of these methods results in hash browns with a crusty surface and meltingly tender bites. As discussed under our Breakfast Burritos (page 26), we often use rendered beef fat, or tallow, for cooking these.

1. Cut the cooled potatoes into slightly uneven bite-size chunks and transfer them to a bowl. In a large skillet over medium heat, melt the tallow or butter and pour about two-thirds of it over the potatoes. Turn off the heat but leave the skillet with its remaining fat on the stove. Stir to coat the potatoes evenly with the fat.

2. Mix together the salt, garlic powder, and pepper. Toss about half of the salt mixture with the potatoes. Scrape the seasoned potato mixture into the skillet, pat into a fairly even layer, and cook over medium heat. Plan on a total cooking time of 10 to 12 minutes, scraping the potatoes up from the bottom a couple of times, so that they brown evenly and form some crispy edges. Taste after a few minutes and add more seasoning, as needed. Serve hot.

Granola

2¾ cups rolled oats

2 cups raw pistachios

1 cup coconut flakes

⅓ cup pumpkin seeds (pepitas)

1 teaspoon kosher salt or coarse sea salt

½ cup packed brown sugar

⅓ cup maple syrup

⅓ cup extra virgin olive oil

1 cup dried cherries

This granola originated with the Eleven Madison Park restaurant, when it was owned by our colleague Danny Meyer. Dinner guests were gifted packages of the granola, created by Chef Daniel Humm, as they finished their meals, to take home for breakfast the next morning. We thought that was a brilliant final bit of hospitality. We also loved the combination of nubbly ingredients, with an excellent balance between the sweet and savory. Our granola, which we offer to folks staying in our Guest Quarters, was inspired by theirs.

1. Heat the oven to 300°F. Line a baking sheet with parchment paper. In a large bowl, combine the oats, pistachios, coconut, pumpkin seeds, and salt. In a small saucepan, warm together the brown sugar, maple syrup, and oil over medium heat. Stir to melt the sugar, then remove from heat, and pour over the oat mixture. Mix well, then pour the granola out onto the baking sheet and spread into an even layer.

2. Bake for 30 to 35 minutes total, until golden, lightly crisp, and fragrant. Stir once about halfway through the baking time. Stir the dried cherries into the granola and let cool. Transfer to jars, bags, or other airtight packaging.

Granola Cookies

MAKES 2½ DOZEN

1¾ cups rolled oats

1 cup raw pistachios

½ cup coconut flakes

½ cup dried cherries

¼ cup pumpkin seeds (pepitas)

1 cup all-purpose flour

1 teaspoon baking powder

1 teaspoon baking soda

1 teaspoon ground cinnamon

¾ teaspoon table salt

½ cup (1 stick) unsalted butter, at room temperature

½ cup packed light brown sugar

½ cup granulated sugar

1 large egg

1 large egg yolk

1 teaspoon pure vanilla extract

These are something like an oatmeal cookie that got dressed up for a date. They have the crunch and tasty bits so loved in granola, but are easier for on-the-go eating during the morning or any other time of day. Because we have so much demand for our granola, we just set aside quantities of its "dry" ingredients to use later to make these cookies. We figure you're more likely to be beginning from scratch though, so the measurements reflect that.

1. Heat the oven to 350°F. Cover 3 baking sheets with parchment paper or silicone mats. Stir together the oats, pistachios, coconut flakes, dried cherries, pumpkin seeds, flour, baking powder, baking soda, cinnamon, and salt in a large bowl. In a medium bowl, combine the butter with the sugars, using a sturdy spoon to mix. Make a well in the middle of the mixture and add to it the egg, egg yolk, and vanilla, stirring them in thoroughly. Scrape this mixture into the large bowl of dry ingredients. Continue stirring until well combined. Cover and refrigerate the dough for 30 minutes.

2. Scoop mounds of dough onto the baking sheets; the mounds should be a bit larger than golf balls. A medium-size ice cream scoop works for this. Leave about 2 inches between the cookies, as they will spread. Bake for 12 to 14 minutes, until medium brown and lightly set. Cool on the baking sheets for at least 10 minutes before transferring to baking racks to cool. The cookies will firm up as they sit.

Waffles

SERVES 4

2½ cups all-purpose flour

1 tablespoon baking powder

1¼ teaspoons table salt

2 large eggs

2 cups whole milk

¼ cup maple syrup, plus more, warmed, for serving

¼ cup granulated sugar

1 tablespoon pure vanilla extract

1 cup (2 sticks) unsalted butter, melted, but cooled briefly; plus more, at room temperature, for serving

People often say our waffles are much more flavorful than most, as well as crisp and light. The secrets are generous quantities of butter, vanilla, baking powder, and maple syrup in the batter itself. They need no adornment beyond more butter and maple syrup, but they can be gussied up with toppings of berries, candied pecans, chocolate chips, caramel sauce, whipped cream, a dusting of confectioners' sugar, or pretty much whatever you want. You might also try pairing the waffles with The Judge's Fried Chicken (page 180).

1. Mix together the flour, baking powder, and salt in a medium bowl. Set aside.

2. In a large bowl, whisk together the eggs and milk. Once combined, whisk in the maple syrup, sugar, and vanilla. Pour in the melted and cooled butter and whisk again. Stir in the dry ingredients, mixing until just barely combined. You'll have a few lumps. That's fine.

3. Heat a well-greased waffle iron. Cook waffles one at a time, following the directions from the waffle-iron manufacturer. They should be crisp and brown when done.

4. Serve the waffles individually as they are ready or hold them briefly in a warm oven until all are finished. Offer them with additional butter and syrup, or some of the topping options mentioned above.

Fruit Salad with Honey-Lemon Dressing

SERVES 4 OR MORE

HONEY-LEMON DRESSING

¼ cup plus 2 tablespoons honey

¼ cup plus 2 tablespoons fresh lemon juice (from about 3 large lemons)

2 cups blueberries

1 pound strawberries, green stems removed, quartered

1 large banana, diced in neat bite-size pieces

1 apple such as Honeycrisp or Red Delicious, diced in neat bite-size pieces

1 or 2 peaches or a small mango, peeled, pitted, and diced, or a handful or green or red grapes, halved, optional

This is a great salad to help use up various fruit that you might have on hand. We typically have a mix of berries and bananas, with apples for crunch. Cubes of mango or some Central Texas peaches are great additions, as are a mix of halved grapes for more color. Everyone always thinks the dressing must be much more complicated than it is, a simple blend of honey with lemon juice.

1. Make the dressing, whisking together the honey and lemon juice in a large bowl. Add the fruit and stir together well. Spoon into bowls or, for a fancier affair, martini glasses, and serve.

French-Fried French Toast

SERVES 4 OR MORE

Butter or vegetable oil spray

TOPPING

¼ cup confectioners' sugar

1 tablespoon ground cinnamon

8 slices soft white bread, such as Mrs. Baird's, sliced into halves or thirds

2 cups pancake mix, such as Birch Benders or Bisquick Original Pancake and Baking Mix

2 cups whole milk

1 large egg

Vegetable oil, for frying

Cane syrup or maple syrup, for serving

Here's a gem, something we concocted for a late-night breakfast after a wedding we catered in Henderson, Texas. On the same weekend, the town was celebrating its Cane Syrup Festival, so that was part of the inspiration for a syrup-dunked dish. The French toast has become one of our most popular wedding dishes, but it's just as good as part of a Sunday morning breakfast for family or friends. The frying of this might sound a touch involved, but it gives the French toast a very crisp exterior while the interior is delectably soft. Mrs. Baird's is the Texas white bread of choice, and in fact, a Mrs. Baird's sign emblazons the Steakhouse's front screen door. Serve cane syrup or maple syrup in ramekins so that the fingers of French toast can be dunked into it.

1. Heat the oven to 300°F. Butter a baking sheet or mist it with vegetable oil spray. Line another baking sheet with paper towels, place a baking rack over it, and place it near the cooktop.

2. Stir together the topping ingredients in a small bowl and reserve. Cut each bread slice into 2 or 3 strips.

3. Whisk together the pancake mix, milk, and egg in a large bowl. Dunk several pieces of bread into the batter. Let sit for a minute or so, just long enough for the bread to become saturated without falling apart.

4. Warm about 2 inches of oil in a deep 12- to 14-inch cast-iron skillet over medium heat to 350°F.

5. Let excess batter drip off, then lay the bread in the oil. Briefly cook, about 1 to 1½ minutes per side, turning once, until golden brown. Remove with tongs to the baking rack to drain. Then transfer the finished French toast to the buttered baking sheet and place in the oven while you prepare the remaining French toast. When all toast is cooked, arrange on plates or a platter and dust with the topping mixture. Serve hot with ramekins of syrup for dunking.

Italian Sausage and Cheese Strata

SERVES 6

One 1- to 1¼-pound loaf country or sourdough bread, crusts removed if thick

1¼ cups (about 5 ounces) grated fontina or Muenster cheese, or another good melting cheese

1½ cups small-curd cottage cheese, or more of the cheese you chose above

12 ounces bulk Italian sausage, fried until well browned

5 large eggs

1 cup milk or half-and-half

1 teaspoon dry mustard or Dijon mustard

½ teaspoon table salt

Freshly ground black pepper

2 tablespoons salted butter, melted

2 tablespoons extra virgin olive oil

A strata, sometimes called an overnight casserole or by more whimsical names such as a featherbed, is great for making ahead. Layers of bread and an egg mixture are combined with other flavorings, such as this combo honoring Tom's Italian heritage. If your market doesn't carry bulk Italian sausage, buy links and simply squeeze the meat out of the casings before frying.

1. Oil or butter a deep 9- to 10-inch baking dish. Slice the bread about ½ inch thick. Arrange 2 to 3 alternating layers of the bread, grated cheese, cottage cheese, and sausage in the baking dish. Cut or tear bread slices if needed to make snug layers.

2. Whisk the eggs with the milk, mustard, salt, and pepper. Pour the custard over the bread mixture. Mix together the butter and oil and drizzle over the mixture. Cover and refrigerate the strata for at least 1 hour and up to overnight. Remove the strata from the refrigerator 20 to 30 minutes before you plan to bake it.

3. Heat the oven to 350°F. Bake the strata for 50 to 55 minutes, until puffed, golden brown, and lightly set at the center. Serve hot.

CAST-IRON COOKERY— AT HOME ON OUR RANGE

Tom has always been a collector, and he's amassed quite a variety of vintage cast-iron—the pots and pans and Dutch ovens used on the range. Some of these finds are a part of our home kitchen today. Isaac Morton, founder of Smithey Ironware, started in a fashion like Tom, collecting old rusty skillets and other pieces, and restoring them to their 19th-century glory. Eventually, Isaac decided there might be a market for new cast-iron cookware honoring the classic style of the old pieces, but using modern technology. Smithey Ironware was born. The line has expanded to include carbon steel cookware, which was developed working with his neighbor, the renowned blacksmith Robert Thomas. We proudly carry both Smithey cast-iron and carbon steel cookware in our Perini Ranch Country Market and online at periniranch.com. The cookware is as beautiful as it is functional, in the kitchen or over the campfire.

A BATCH OF BLOODYS

Festive mornings can be for mimosas, but here on the ranch, it's the Bloody Mary and its kin that rule the day. We use plenty of horseradish and Worcestershire, and garnish with pickled okra for a Texas touch. Our Steak Rub rims the glasses, and our Beef Sticks, created from tenderloin trimmings, make the perfect stirrer for any of these drinks. Both can be ordered from periniranch. com. The vodka of preference here is Tito's from just down the road in Austin. These are easy cocktails to batch for a breakfast or brunch gathering.

Our Bloody Mary

SERVES 1

Celery salt

1 ounce vodka

5 ounces tomato juice

½ teaspoon prepared horseradish

1 ½ teaspoons Worcestershire sauce

Salt and pepper

3 to 4 dashes of Tabasco

1 pickled okra

1. Moisten the rim of a glass and coat it with celery salt. Place the vodka, tomato juice, and horseradish in a container and stir until well combined. Fill the rimmed glass with ice and pour the vodka mixture over it. Add the Worcestershire sauce and Tabasco, season with salt, pepper, and celery salt, and gently stir. Garnish with pickled okra and serve.

THE BLOODY MARIA: Substitute tequila (we prefer silver) for the vodka.

A PITCHER OF BLOODYS: Rim glasses with celery salt. In a 2-quart pitcher, combine 1½ cups vodka, 6 cups tomato juice, and 3 tablespoons prepared horseradish. Add ½ cup Worcestershire sauce, season with salt, pepper, and celery salt, and gently stir. Pour over ice and garnish with pickled okra.

IT'S A BLOODY SHAME: Called a Virgin Mary sometimes, the cocktail morphs easily into a mocktail. Just leave out the vodka or other alcohol and toss in another ice cube or two.

A LITTLE SOMETHING: SAVORY SNACKS & COCKTAILS

One-bite wonders, that's what we often call these little bar snacks, or nibbles that can precede a sit-down meal. Some are a bit more substantial, when you're feeding cowboys coming in from a day on the range. We finish the chapter with a few favorite libations. The nibbles and drinks will help get any evening off to a delicious start.

Jalapeño Bites

MAKES 2 DOZEN

One 8-ounce package cream cheese, at room temperature, cut into 12 pieces

6 medium jalapeños, each sliced in half lengthwise and seeded

12 thick slices bacon, cut in half

24 toothpicks

Our Jalapeño Bites represent one of our proudest success stories. Not only are they our most popular Perini Ranch Steakhouse appetizer, but they are assembled by a special Abilene organization, Disability Resources Inc. (DRI), a local residence for folks with intellectual disabilities. We deliver our ingredients to DRI, whose clients precisely assemble these spicy, savory bites. Every December we celebrate this successful partnership with a big party at the Steakhouse. We serve some 200 dozen of these every single week.

1. Heat the oven to 375°F. Line a baking sheet with parchment paper or a silicone mat.

2. Put a piece of cream cheese into each jalapeño half. Cut each cream cheese–filled portion in half crosswise. (This is easier than trying to fill 24 jalapeño pieces.) Wrap each quarter with a piece of bacon and secure with a toothpick. Arrange the bites on the prepared pan.

3. Bake for 18 to 22 minutes, until the bacon is crisp and the cream cheese is melted. Serve warm.

Spicy Pecans

MAKES 2 CUPS

2 tablespoons salted butter

1 tablespoon Worcestershire sauce

1 tablespoon chili powder

¼ teaspoon garlic powder

¼ teaspoon cayenne

¼ teaspoon table salt, or more to taste

2 cups pecans

We've discovered that our steak rub has a multitude of uses. For instance, we use it instead of salt to coat the glass rim for our Bloody Mary. We give credit to Tom's daughter Caroline, who came up with the idea of sprinkling some rub on fresh or grilled pineapple. And then there are these toasted piquant pecans to serve with cocktails.

1. Heat the oven to 350°F. Line a baking sheet with parchment paper or a silicone mat.

2. Melt the butter in a medium skillet over medium heat. Stir in the Worcestershire sauce, chili powder, garlic powder, cayenne, and salt. When combined, add the pecans and stir to coat them well. Arrange the pecans in a single layer on the prepared baking sheet.

3. Bake for 8 to 10 minutes, then stir the nuts and bake for an additional 8 to 10 minutes, until the pecans are dry and toasted. Serve warm or at room temperature. Store in a zippered plastic bag for 2 to 3 days.

Rosemary Marcona Almonds

MAKES 2 CUPS

2 tablespoons extra virgin olive oil

Two 2- or 3-inch sprigs rosemary, plus 1 tablespoon minced

2 cups (about ¾ pound) Marcona almonds

Kosher salt or other coarse salt

Marcona almonds, almost exclusively grown in Spain, are creamier in taste and moister in texture than the more common California almond. They make an excellent cocktail snack, especially with a bit of rosemary scenting them. We like these on their own or as a part of a charcuterie platter. Pairing the almonds with a glass of cava, the Spanish sparkler, or a glass of Rioja, is a nice touch, but they're darned good with a Shiner Bock or a local craft beer too.

1. Warm the oil with 1 rosemary sprig in a medium skillet over medium-low heat. Let the mixture cook together for 2 to 3 minutes.

2. Stir in the almonds, coating them with the oil mixture. Cook them for about 10 minutes, stirring several times, until golden and fragrant. Discard the rosemary sprig, and toss the almonds with the minced rosemary and salt to taste.

3. Transfer the nuts to a bowl. Garnish with the remaining sprig and serve.

Trash Mix

MAKES ABOUT 20 CUPS

4 cups Rice Chex

4 cups Corn Chex

4 cups Wheat Chex

4 cups Cheerios

4 cups thin pretzel sticks

1 heaping cup pecan halves

6 tablespoons beef tallow or bacon drippings

6 tablespoons (¾ stick) unsalted butter

2 teaspoons garlic salt

1 teaspoon onion powder

2 tablespoons Worcestershire sauce

1 tablespoon plus 1 teaspoon liquid smoke

1 teaspoon Tabasco

Our friend and colleague Kay Morris along with her husband, Mike, worked with us tirelessly for decades until their recent retirement. Kay first put together this particular twist on the perennial favorite, Chex party mix, usually referred to in Texas as "trash." It's a recipe that everyone tinkers with a bit to taste. Just use plenty of the seasoning-and-tallow-butter mixture. Though bacon drippings have deep flavor, we use our rendered beef tallow whenever possible. Tallow can be bought from many butchers as well as a number of sources online.

1. Heat the oven to 250°F. Combine the Chex cereals, Cheerios, pretzels, and pecans in a roasting pan.

2. Melt the beef tallow and butter together in a small saucepan over medium-low heat. Stir in the garlic salt, followed by the remaining ingredients. Pour the mixture over the cereals and stir until evenly coated.

3. Bake 45 minutes, stirring twice at 15-minute intervals. Spread the mixture on paper towels to cool and serve.

Marinated Olives

MAKES ABOUT 2½ CUPS

¼ cup extra virgin olive oil

2 tablespoons red wine vinegar

5 bay leaves

2 garlic cloves, thinly sliced

Strips of zest from 1 lemon

1 tablespoon fresh thyme sprigs

½ tablespoon fresh rosemary

½ teaspoon fennel seeds

1 cup imported green olives, such as Castelvetrano

1 cup imported black olives, such as Kalamata

We love this mix of olives, loaded with fragrant herbs, as a nibble at cocktail hour. If you can find pitted olives, that makes for even easier nibbling. Let the olives sit in the aromatic mixture for at least a couple of hours, or up to a couple of weeks. Give the jar a good shake now and then to redistribute the seasonings. And always keep a batch on hand for impromptu gatherings.

1. Combine the oil, vinegar, bay leaves, and garlic in a small saucepan. Warm over low heat just until the mixture starts to become fragrant. Remove from the heat and stir in the lemon zest, thyme, rosemary, and fennel seeds.

2. Spoon the olives into a wide-mouth jar. Pour the oil-vinegar mixture over the olives. Shake the jar well to distribute the seasonings. Refrigerate for at least 2 hours or up to a couple of weeks.

Blue Cheese–Topped Dried Apricots with Hot Honey

MAKES 2 DOZEN

4 ounces Danish blue cheese crumbles, or other mild flavored blue cheese, at room temperature

1 ounce cream cheese, at room temperature

24 plump dried apricots

24 walnut halves

2 to 3 tablespoons hot honey

Sweet, salty, tangy, and altogether delectable. If you have no hot honey, substitute a drizzle of your favorite honey and sprinkle a dash of cayenne over the top of the finished apricots.

1. Mix together the blue cheese and cream cheese in a small bowl. Mound a generous teaspoon of the mixture over each apricot. Press a walnut half into the cheese and arrange all of the apricots on a platter. Just before serving, drizzle each one with about ¼ teaspoon of honey.

BLUE CHEESE-TOPPED DRIED APRICOTS WITH HOT HONEY

SEE PAGE 57

Pico de Gallo

MAKES ABOUT 2½ CUPS

1 cup diced tomatoes

½ cup diced yellow onion

1 to 3 jalapeños, seeded and minced

½ teaspoon kosher salt, or more to taste

1 teaspoon fresh lime juice

1 tablespoon chopped fresh cilantro leaves

Tortilla Chips (page 62)

Folks around here consider pico de gallo, a fresh chunky jalapeño-fueled salsa, to be the official condiment of Tex-Mex cooking. To make a quality version, start with the best vine-ripened tomatoes you can find at a farmers' market or grow your own, like we do. Take the time to cut the tomatoes and onions in similar size pieces, so you get a taste of both in every bite. Start with one jalapeño; add more as desired.

For a cocktail party, make pico de gallo, guacamole, and queso, and serve the trio with a hefty basket of homemade tortilla chips and plenty of Ranch Water and Mesquite-a-Rita cocktails. Pico de gallo can also be spooned on tacos, scrambled eggs, pinto beans, or even burgers.

1. Mix together the tomatoes, onion, and jalapeños in a bowl. Stir in the salt and lime juice and refrigerate for at least 30 minutes. Just before serving, mix in the cilantro and taste for salt, adding more as necessary.

2. Serve with chips.

Guacamole

MAKES 3 CUPS

3 ripe Hass avocados, pitted and peeled

½ cup Pico de Gallo (opposite page)

1½ tablespoons fresh lime juice

½ teaspoon kosher salt

Tortilla Chips (page 62)

The cocktail hour is a very special time of the day at our home. Even though we live together and work together, many days we don't see each other until we meet for drinks around 5:00 p.m. If we lose track of time, our basset hounds, Jett, Winston, and Oliver, remind us that it's cocktail time. We all head to the patio with a drink and snack in hand to review the day's activities and make our dinner plans. Often as not, we choose the simple delight of guacamole with warm, homemade chips. We use Hass avocados, the nubby, dark-green-almost-black variety, for their creaminess. The flesh should yield lightly when you press the fruit with your thumb.

1. Mash the avocados in a bowl with a large fork but leave some small chunks for texture. Gently stir in the pico de gallo, lime juice, and salt. Serve with tortilla chips within 30 minutes of preparation.

TORTILLA CHIPS

Of course, you can buy tortilla chips to go with guacamole, queso, pico de gallo, cactus salsa, and other dips, but they're easy to make and taste so much better.

   Cut a dozen thin, 6-inch corn tortillas into quarters. Attach a deep-fry thermometer to the side of a deep, heavy skillet or a Dutch oven. Pour 2 inches of vegetable oil into the skillet and heat to 375°F. Set a wire baking rack over some paper towels near the stovetop. Put 6 to 8 tortilla wedges in the oil and cook for just a few seconds. As soon as the chips are crisp, but not brown, scoop them out with a slotted spoon and drain on the rack. Sprinkle with coarse salt while hot. Repeat with the remaining tortilla wedges, salting as you go. Serve in a napkin-lined basket.

   Tortilla chips can be stored for a couple of days in an airtight container. Rewarm the chips on a baking sheet in a 250°F oven for a couple of minutes.

Cactus Salsa

MAKES ABOUT 4 CUPS

One 15.5-ounce jar nopales or nopalitos, drained, rinsed, and diced

One 6-ounce fresh nopal (prickly pear cactus pad), stickers removed, diced

1 cup diced fresh tomatoes

½ cup diced white onion

2 tablespoons extra virgin olive oil

2 tablespoons minced pickled jalapeño

1 tablespoon minced fresh cilantro leaves

½ teaspoon crumbled dried Mexican oregano

½ teaspoon kosher salt, or more to taste

Tortilla Chips (page 62)

When we serve this exotic prickly pear salsa, it always elicits positive comments even from folks who didn't grow up in cactus country. The recipe comes from our friends at Mi Tierra Café y Panaderia, a truly iconic San Antonio restaurant since 1941. When we were served the salsa at the chef's table one evening, we became obsessed!

We like the combination of fresh cactus pads with the tangier, softer textured ones from a jar. You'll typically find both in a store that has a large selection of Mexican items. In some cases, the fresh cactus pad (a nopal) will be sold whole with all of its thorns removed. In larger markets, you may see huge round towers, taller than eye level, of whole nopales piled up. Some places offer fresh, already-sliced nopales (nopalitos). And yes, you could score a wild cactus pad in much of the American Southwest. However, those are covered in fine stickers that you probably don't want to mess with.

1. Combine the jarred nopales, fresh nopal, tomatoes, onion, olive oil, jalapeño, cilantro, oregano, and salt in a bowl. Taste and add more salt, if you wish. Refrigerate for 30 minutes. Serve with Tortilla Chips.

Chile con Queso

MAKES ABOUT 4 CUPS

½ pound bulk hot pork sausage

½ cup diced onion

1 cup Ro-Tel Original Diced Tomatoes & Green Chilies

1 pound Velveeta, cut into 2-inch pieces

Tortilla Chips (page 62)

In Texas, chile con queso—or just queso—is considered its own food group. Yes, queso is right up there with chili and chicken-fried steak. People are always trying to improve on this cheese and sausage dip by omitting the Velveeta or stirring in some fancy cheeses that just don't belong. Sometimes you just have to put aside any pretensions of food snobbery and go with what works.

A little-known fact about queso is that leftovers freeze beautifully, but usually there are no leftovers.

1. Combine the sausage and onion in a skillet over medium heat. Cook, using a wooden spoon to break up the sausage, until the sausage is brown and crisp and the onion is soft. If the sausage renders more than a table-spoon of fat, discard it. Stir in the Diced Tomatoes & Green Chilies and Velveeta. Cook over low heat, stirring frequently, until the Velveeta is melted and the mixture is hot and bubbly. Serve the queso right from the skillet, or spoon into a heatproof bowl that can be placed on a warming tray. The queso can also be kept warm in a slow cooker. Serve with chips.

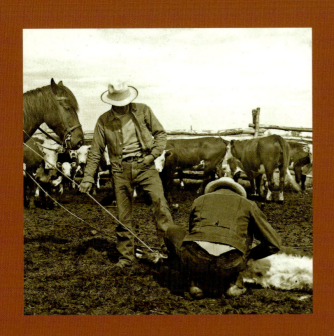

CALF FRIES

Historically, calf fries have been a favorite at ranch events. Considered quite the delicacy, they are difficult to explain in polite company. When we passed them as an hors d'oeuvre before dinner at New York's James Beard House, some guests were surprised to learn that calf fries are bull testicles. Others preferred not to know the provenance of the tender fried bits they enjoyed.

Calf fries are available fresh during the spring and early summer (frozen the rest of the year), when cowboys brand, castrate, and vaccinate calves. Once the outer membranes are removed, Tom quarters them, dusts them in seasoned flour, and deep-fries them until golden brown. If requested in advance, we're happy to offer them at the Steakhouse or at private events.

When our co-author Cheryl shared her story of attending a ranch branding, cooking fresh testicles on a shovel over a wood fire, and then devouring them, we knew we'd found the right person to work with us on this book.

Goat Cheese Crostini, Two Ways

MAKES 2 DOZEN

½ baguette, cut into 24 rounds, each about ¼-inch thick

Extra virgin olive oil

4 ounces creamy fresh goat cheese

2 ounces cream cheese

1 teaspoon minced fresh flat-leaf parsley

1 teaspoon minced fresh thyme or ½ teaspoon crumbled dried thyme

1 teaspoon grated lemon zest

¼ teaspoon kosher salt

¼ teaspoon ground black pepper

Minced chives or jalapeño jelly, or both

Oh, how we love goat cheese around here. These crostini are easy to plate or pass around at a fancier event. A sprinkling of chives is pretty, especially when our chives are flowering and we can garnish the serving platter with the purple blossoms. A dot of jalapeño jelly combines well with the cheese mixture too, so serve them up either way. Both the crostini toasts and the goat cheese topping can be made up to two days ahead.

1. Heat the oven to 400°F. Arrange the bread slices on a baking sheet and brush with oil. Bake the bread slices until golden, 4 to 5 minutes. Keep a close eye on them though, to make sure they don't burn. Set aside to cool.

2. In a food processor, blend together the goat cheese and cream cheese until combined and smooth. Sprinkle in the parsley, thyme, lemon zest, salt, and pepper. Pulse to just blend everything together.

3. Within about 30 minutes of when you plan to serve the crostini, mound the cheese mixture evenly over the toasts. Top each with either a sprinkling of chives or a dollop of jelly—or dress half of the crostini with both of them—and serve.

Cheddar-Pecan Cheese Straws

MAKES ABOUT 4 DOZEN

½ cup (1 stick) salted butter, at room temperature

4 ounces sharp Cheddar cheese, shredded and at room temperature

1¼ cups all-purpose flour

½ teaspoon kosher salt

½ teaspoon cayenne

½ cup finely chopped pecans

Originally, these buttery crackers were called straws because they were piped from a pastry bag and cut into 2- to 3-inch straws. These are rounds, with the dough rolled into a log and sliced. Because of Lisa's South Carolina roots, cheese straws are a must at any gathering. Our recipe is a variation of a recipe from the Junior League of Abilene. (Yes, Texans like cheese straws, too.) You can double the recipe, bake, and store them in the freezer, so they're always on hand for cocktail hour.

1. Place the butter and cheese in the bowl of a stand mixer and cream on high speed for several minutes, until completely blended. Stop the mixer, scrape down the sides, and add the flour, salt, and cayenne. Beat again on medium speed until the dry ingredients are incorporated. Scrape the dough out onto a work surface. Scatter the pecans over the dough and work them into the dough.

2. Divide and roll the dough into two logs, about the diameter of a quarter. Roll the logs in wax paper and twist the ends. Chill thoroughly in the refrigerator for at least 2 hours or up to a week. (Well-wrapped logs can be frozen up to 1 month. Let them come to room temperature before slicing.)

3. Heat the oven to 350°F. Line 2 baking sheets with parchment paper. Cut the logs into ¼-inch-thick slices. Rotate the dough one-quarter turn after slicing about a half-dozen straws, to keep the shape even, repeating as needed. Arrange the straws about ½ inch apart on the lined baking sheets. Bake for 8 to 10 minutes, just until set and golden. Serve warm or at room temperature. Store in a tin or other covered container for up to 1 week.

Pickled Okra with Pimento Cheese

MAKES 18

PIMENTO CHEESE

½ cup mayonnaise

6 ounces cream cheese, at room temperature

¼ teaspoon table salt

⅛ teaspoon freshly ground black pepper

One 3- to 4-ounce jar pimentos, drained and diced

¾ pound (3 cups) shredded (on large holes of a grater) sharp Cheddar cheese

¼ teaspoon red pepper flakes, or more to taste

One 16-ounce jar pickled okra, drained

These two iconic Southern specialties pair surprisingly well. You can buy already-made pimento cheese or make this version of Southern comfort food. The recipe yields enough pimento cheese that you'll have some left over to spread on crackers or use on sandwiches.

1. **To Make the Pimento Cheese:** Cream together the mayonnaise and cream cheese in a medium bowl until well combined. Stir in the salt and pepper. Add the pimentos and Cheddar and stir together gently. You want some texture remaining. Add red pepper flakes to taste. Refrigerate, covered, for at least 30 minutes or up to several days. Makes 2½ cups.

2. **To Fill the Okra:** Slice down one side of each okra pod from near tip to tail. At the broader stem end, make a small cut perpendicular to the long slit so that you have cut a "T." Gently scrape out the okra seeds. Nudge about 1 teaspoon pimento cheese into the okra and neatly mound another 1 teaspoon on top. Repeat with remaining okra and cheese, using about ¾ cup of the cheese. Serve right away or cover and refrigerate for up to several hours.

Stuffed BLTs

MAKES 2 DOZEN

24 plump cherry tomatoes or other bite-size tomatoes

4 slices bacon, finely diced

3 to 4 tablespoons Buttermilk Ranch Dressing (page 100)

½ cup packed finely shredded then diced romaine or iceberg lettuce

Kosher salt

Some of our customers call these tomato poppers, since the tomatoes are stuffed with BLT fixings: Hollowed-out cherry tomatoes are filled with the classic sandwich's signature flavors. It's summer in one bite.

1. Slice a tiny sliver off the bottom of each tomato, so they will sit flat on a tray. Then slice off about ¼ of the tomato top. Using a small spoon, like a ¼-teaspoon measuring spoon, hollow out the tomatoes. (Tomato tops and interiors can go into salsa, soup, or tomato sauce.)

2. Put the diced bacon in a cold skillet. Turn the heat to medium-low and cook the bacon for 5 to 7 minutes, until brown and crisp. Remove the bacon with a slotted spoon and drain on paper towels.

3. Mix together 3 tablespoons of the ranch dressing with the bacon and lettuce. Salt to taste. Add the rest of the dressing to the mixture if it seems dry. Using a teaspoon, fill each tomato cavity, mounding up the filling. Serve immediately or cover with plastic wrap and refrigerate for up to several hours.

Praline Bacon

MAKES 10 SLICES

Vegetable oil spray

⅓ cup pecans

⅓ cup (not packed) brown sugar

10 thick slices bacon

3 tablespoons 100 percent pure cane syrup or light corn syrup

We created this sweet, smoky, salty, crunchy treat for a couple who wanted an elaborate cocktail party instead of a sit-down dinner for their wedding reception. The crisp bacon strips were arranged standing up in wooden boxes and placed on bars throughout the party site. Be sure to grind the pecans finely so they stick to the bacon but are still recognizable as pecans. Make a double batch; they disappear in no time.

1. Heat the oven to 350°F. Line a baking sheet with parchment paper or a silicone mat. Mist a wire baking rack with vegetable oil spray and place it on the baking sheet.

2. Toast the pecans in a dry skillet over medium-low heat, stirring often so they don't burn, until they are aromatic. Set aside to cool for 5 to 10 minutes. Combine the pecans and brown sugar in a food processor and pulse until the nuts are finely chopped.

3. Arrange the bacon slices on the wire rack. Bake for 10 to 12 minutes. The bacon will not be fully cooked at this point. Using paper towels, blot the bacon to remove any excess fat. Brush the tops of each bacon slice well with the cane syrup. Evenly sprinkle the pecan-sugar mixture on the bacon slices. Return the bacon to the oven and bake for 15 minutes, or until the bacon is crisp and the topping has melted. Let the bacon strips sit and firm up, so they can stand without support. Serve at room temperature.

OUR TENDERLOIN'S ORIGIN STORY

In 1995, we were asked to cook dinner at the James Beard House in New York City for the James Beard Foundation's patrons. It's like an actor being nominated for an Academy Award. After we recovered from the initial shock and said yes, the reality of the expenses we would incur started to sink in. We would need to fly key staff to New York, put them up in hotels for several days, and donate all the food.

It was suggested to us that we might offset some of the cost if we could generate some Steakhouse publicity with New York media while in town. So, we shipped a few of our Mesquite Smoked Peppered Beef Tenderloins to food writers at magazines and the *New York Times* in hopes of snagging their attention. No one seemed interested until a call came from the *Times*, asking us to ship them a second tenderloin. The *Times* staffer making the request was so vague about why the newspaper wanted another one that Tom suspected someone just wanted it for their personal enjoyment. He considered not sending the tenderloin, but, in the end, shipped the beef as requested.

When another call came from someone talking about fact checking, Tom thought he was asking about checking our fax machine. After an awkward minute, it became clear that this fact-checker wanted details about our toll-free number and other mail-order specifics. Our tenderloin was a couple of days away from being named the *New York Times* mail-order gift of the year! Our beef had made its way to the paper's committee overseeing the selection of the best holiday gifts. The only problem was that we had no USDA-approved facility to process the tenderloins and no mail-order system for large-scale shipping. You can bet, however, that Tom figured out both right away. He's never been seen—before or after—moving quite that quickly.

These days, we ship truckloads of Mesquite Smoked Peppered Beef Tenderloins just between Thanksgiving and the end of the year, but they are available all year long. Recently, we interviewed Marian Burros, the *Times* legendary writer from the era, about the tenderloin's selection as the gift of the year all those decades ago. She told us she didn't remember Tom, but she sure still remembered the tenderloin!

Ultimate Four-Cheese Grilled Cheese Sandwich

MAKES 2 SANDWICHES OR 8 APPETIZER PORTIONS

SPECIAL SAUCE

½ cup mayonnaise

2 tablespoons Dijon mustard

2 tablespoons grated Parmesan cheese

½ teaspoon kosher salt or other coarse salt

¼ teaspoon ground white pepper

About 2 tablespoons salted butter, at room temperature

4 slices multi-grain bread

¼ cup (about 1 ounce) grated medium yellow Cheddar cheese

¼ cup (about 1 ounce) grated medium white Cheddar cheese

¼ cup (about 1 ounce) grated Gruyère cheese

This grilled cheese sandwich makes a full lunch for a pair of diners but, because it's fairly rich, we often cut it into quarters to serve as an appetizer. It's the accompanying "special sauce" that puts it over the top. While plain old white bread makes a darned good classic grilled cheese, this version requires slices with a bit of heft to them. Our Gap Café serves the sandwiches on multi-grain bread, but sourdough works well too.

1. Stir together the sauce ingredients in a small bowl.

2. Spread the butter over one side of each bread slice. On the other side of each slice, spread a generous amount of sauce. Lay each slice on a work surface. Combine the two Cheddars and the Gruyère. Top two of the bread slices with equal portions of the cheese mixture. Top each sandwich, buttered side up, with a bread slice.

3. Transfer the sandwiches to a heavy skillet and warm over medium heat. Cook until the sandwiches are golden brown on both sides, with melting cheese, about 10 minutes total, turning them as necessary. Cut each sandwich in half or into quarters and serve, piled up decoratively if serving as appetizers.

Grilled Provolone and Chimichurri

SERVES 4 OR MORE

CHIMICHURRI

1 small bunch fresh parsley, stems discarded

1 small bunch fresh cilantro, stems discarded

1 teaspoon crumbled dried oregano

2 garlic cloves, sliced thin

¾ cup extra virgin olive oil

¼ cup red wine vinegar

¼ cup water

2 teaspoons red pepper flakes, or more to taste

1 tablespoon kosher salt, or more to taste

1 pound provolone cheese, cut into slices that are at least 1 inch thick

1 teaspoon red pepper flakes

½ teaspoon crumbled dried oregano

Toasted baguette slices, for serving

There are really not many things better than melted cheese. Fondue, queso fundido, or this Argentinian-inspired provolone with tangy herb sauce, inspired by Chef Francis Mallman's visit here for our Buffalo Gap Wine & Food Summit a few years ago. Chimichurri, Argentina's well-known sauce for steak, also pairs well with tangy provolone cheese. Unlike some mixtures of fresh herbs, the "chimi" can be made a day or more ahead. We like to serve this in individual 6-inch cast-iron skillets, but presenting it in one large pan is quite striking too.

1. Prepare the chimichurri, combining all of the ingredients in a food processor and pureeing. Spoon into a bowl to use immediately or cover and refrigerate for up to several days.

2. Heat the broiler. Place the cheese in a cast-iron skillet. Sprinkle with the pepper flakes and oregano. Place the skillet under the broiler briefly until the cheese is melted and bubbly, with a few appetizing brown spots, about 5 minutes. Watch it very carefully though, to avoid turning it into rubber.

3. Serve the cheese from the skillet, its hot handle covered with a towel or napkin. Accompany with the chimichurri and baguette slices.

TOM'S TIP: A fun accompaniment for the melted cheese and chimichurri is our Perini Ranch beef sticks. Buy them at our Country Market or from periniranch.com.

Smoked Salmon
Potato Chips

MAKES ABOUT 2 DOZEN

One 6.5-ounce bag potato chips

4 ounces (½ cup) crème fraîche

4 ounces thinly sliced smoked salmon, cut into 1-inch pieces

6 large fresh dill sprigs, divided into 24 fronds

Creamy. Crunchy. Salty. Smooth. Sophisticated. Put these easy appetizers together at the last minute. And keep in mind that you need sturdy potato chips, such as Boulder Canyon's Sea Salt and Cracked Pepper Chips, to hold the salmon and crème fraîche.

1. Pour the potato chips onto a baking sheet and pick out 24 of the largest, best-looking ones. Save the rest for munching. Spoon a dollop of crème fraîche on top of each chip, followed by a square of smoked salmon.

2. Garnish with a dill frond and serve immediately.

Caviar Pie

SERVES 8 TO 12

Vegetable oil spray

6 large eggs, hard-boiled, peeled, and chopped fine

3 to 4 tablespoons mayonnaise

Kosher salt and freshly ground black pepper

¾ cup minced sweet or red onion, rinsed and drained on paper towels

One 14-ounce can water-packed artichoke hearts, drained and chopped fine

8 ounces cream cheese, at room temperature

⅔ cup sour cream

Two 2-ounce jars whitefish caviar

Crackers, cucumber slices, or toast, for serving

Initially popular in the 1980s, this retro dish made a splash in our area thanks to a recipe from the Junior League of Abilene. Theoretically, it serves up to a dozen folks, but it always seems to disappear too quickly, no matter the number of friends digging into it.

1. Mist the bottom and sides of an 8-inch springform pan with vegetable oil spray.

2. In a medium bowl, stir together the eggs and 3 tablespoons of the mayonnaise. If the mixture seems dry, stir in more mayonnaise, up to the remaining tablespoon. Season with salt and pepper. Spoon the mixture into the pan and smooth the surface with a rubber spatula. Top with the onion, followed by the artichokes.

3. In another bowl, stir together the cream cheese and sour cream until well combined. Spoon the mixture over the artichokes, and smooth it. Cover the pan and refrigerate it for at least 2 hours and up to overnight.

4. Shortly before serving, rinse the caviar and drain it gently. Arrange it over the top. Serve with crackers, cucumbers, toast, or other dippers.

Fried Quail Legs

MAKES 1 DOZEN

Vegetable oil, for frying

2 large eggs

¾ cup whole milk

1 teaspoon table salt

12 quail legs

1¼ cups all-purpose flour

¼ cup Cajun seasoning

Quail are a big deal in our part of Texas, especially in the fall when people come from all over the world to hunt the diminutive birds. We serve farm-raised quail from Ingram, Texas. You can order quail legs online or ask your butcher to order them. Each quail leg comes with the thigh attached, so you get a couple of delicious bites from each one.

1. Clip a deep-fry thermometer to the inside of a deep 12- or 14-inch cast-iron skillet or Dutch oven. Pour in the oil to a depth of 3 inches and bring the temperature of the oil to 350°F over medium-high heat. Line a baking sheet with paper towels. Put a wire baking rack on top of the paper towels.

2. Whisk together the eggs, milk, and salt in a bowl. Add the quail legs to the egg wash, stirring to coat all of them. Combine the flour and Cajun seasoning on a shallow plate. One by one, dip the quail legs lightly in the flour mixture and shake each to eliminate any excess flour.

3. In batches, fry the quail legs in the hot oil until golden brown, about 4 minutes. Don't crowd the pot or else the temperature of the oil will drop, and the quail legs won't be crisp. Use tongs to transfer the quail legs to the wire rack. Repeat with the remaining quail legs. Serve hot.

Marinated Shrimp

2 tablespoons crab boil dry spice blend, such as Zatarain's

1 pound (26 to 30 per pound) medium shrimp, peeled, deveined, and tails removed

½ medium red onion, thinly sliced into rings

¾ cup white or apple cider vinegar

½ cup vegetable oil

¼ cup granulated sugar

¾ teaspoon celery seeds

¾ teaspoon kosher salt

2 tablespoons capers, plus 1 to 2 tablespoons caper brine

While Lisa's Lowcountry South Carolina heritage is the source of many of our seafood recipes, others come from the Texas Gulf Coast. This one evolved from a customer's Mexican ceviche recipe.

1. Combine the spice blend and 6 cups cold water in a large saucepan. Bring to a boil over high heat. Add the shrimp and return to a boil. As soon as the shrimp turn pink and opaque, 2 to 3 minutes, drain them in a colander and rinse under cold water for 10 seconds.

2. When cool enough to handle, alternately layer the shrimp and onion in a deep bowl or large jar. In another bowl, whisk together the vinegar, oil, sugar, celery seeds, salt, and capers and their brine. Pour the marinade over the shrimp and onions. Cover with plastic wrap or a lid and refrigerate for at least 6 or up to 12 hours.

3. Arrange the shrimp with some onions and capers on serving plates or in martini glasses and serve chilled.

Mesquite-a-Rita

SERVES 1

Kosher salt

Lime wedge

1½ ounces El Jimador Reposado tequila

1 ounce Housemade Sweet-and-Sour Mix (see below)

½ ounce Grand Marnier orange liqueur

½ ounce Triple Sec orange liqueur

½ ounce fresh lime juice

Lime slice

Here's our signature margarita, one we sell more of than any other drink. Multiply the recipe by the number of friends you have; you can make up to two at a time in a cocktail shaker. We use a well-priced, but high-quality, 100 percent blue agave reposado tequila that has been aged or rested for a couple of months in oak barrels. Just that slight amount of aging rounds and softens the tequila's bite, making it perfect for mixing into cocktails. We use a pair of orange liqueurs and fresh lime juice, never a pre-fab mix for this (or any of our cocktails), making it the ultimate margarita. ¡Salud!

1. Place a thin layer of salt, about 1 tablespoon, on a saucer. Rub the rim of an old-fashioned glass with the lime wedge and dip the rim into the salt. (Omit if you prefer your Margarita *sin sal*, without salt.) Half-fill the glass with cracked ice.

2. Pour the tequila, sweet-and-sour mix, Grand Marnier, Triple Sec, and lime juice into a cocktail shaker. Cover and shake well to combine. Pour over the ice in the glass. Garnish with the lime slice and serve.

HOUSEMADE SWEET-AND-SOUR MIX

This will make more than you need for 1 or 2 margaritas, but refrigerated, it keeps well for at least a week.

MAKES 8 OUNCES

½ cup granulated sugar

½ cup fresh lime juice

½ cup fresh lemon juice

In a small saucepan, bring ½ cup water to a quick boil. Stir in the sugar and continue stirring until the water is clear. Remove from the heat and stir in the lime and lemon juices. Cover and refrigerate until needed.

IT'S ALWAYS TEQUILA TIME IN TEXAS

Given the amount of tequila consumed in Texas, and the burgeoning distilled spirits industry around the state, you could be forgiven if you thought some tequila might be made here. Nope. By law, tequila has to be made in the Mexican state of Jalisco.

While a number of regulations affect its production, a tequila only has to be 51 percent blue agave to be labeled as such. The finest tequilas, though—and the only ones we serve at the Steakhouse—are 100 percent Weber blue agave. The plants, in the family of succulents, shoot out bluish pointed leaves of several feet in length, with rather threatening-looking spines or thorns along the sides and at the tips. *Jimadores*, the source of the El Jimador tequila name in our signature margarita, are men who work the fields, looking for those agaves at the perfect state of ripeness. If under- or overripe, the carbohydrate content will not be right for natural fermentation. They chop off the leaves to uncover the enormous heart of the plant, called a *piña* for its resemblance to a pineapple. Piñas can weigh as much as our trio of basset hounds. It's a laborious project to harvest the piñas, which are baked, mashed or shredded, and then allowed to ferment. The initial tequila produced after distillation is clear, but some are aged in American oak to add more character and a bit of color.

At the Steakhouse, we serve some terrific tequilas, including Maestro Dobel, Codigo by George Strait, Casa Dragones, and Clase Azul, to name just a few.

Ranch Water

SERVES 2

1 lime wedge

1 tablespoon kosher salt

1½ ounces Maestro Dobel Diamante tequila

½ ounce fresh lime juice

Topo Chico or other sparkling water

2 lime wheels

This is a go-to cocktail at the Perini residence. When our friend Kelly Cannon came over one night with a bottle of Maestro Dobel Diamante, it became the signature tequila for ranch water, and has been ever since. Look for Topo Chico, a Mexican sparkling mineral water. If you can't find it, use the fizziest fizzy water you can find. Some evenings it goes down a little too easy . . .

1. Rub a lime wedge around the rim of two old-fashioned glasses and dip the rim of each in the salt. Fill the glasses with ice.

2. Stir the tequila and lime juice in another glass. Divide the mixture between the glasses. Top off each with sparkling water and garnish with a wheel of lime.

WINING & DINING

In 2005, we founded the Buffalo Gap Wine & Food Summit with Dr. Richard and Bunny Becker of Becker Vineyards in Stonewall, Texas, along with Fess Parker of Fess Parker Winery in Los Olivos, California, who grew up in San Angelo before heading off to Hollywood for his acting career. The Summit cultivates the appreciation of fine wine and food through education and industry discussion.

In 2004, Fess was receiving an award in Austin. He flew into Abilene and picked us up, along with dear friend Jimmy Tittle. As we were flying out of Abilene, over Buffalo Gap, Fess said, "You know, Perini Ranch and Buffalo Gap are so interesting, we should do some sort of wine event. And, it should be for people who are serious about wine and food. It should be called a summit."

And, that was about it. Our conversation went on to other things. But Lisa was really intrigued with the idea, so a few days later she called Fess and asked if he was serious about his idea. When he said he was, we decided that with a Texas wine partner, we could conquer the world. Several weeks later, we met in San Antonio and were joined by the Beckers. During a torrential rainstorm that afternoon, we hunkered down with lunch and lots of good wine and founded the Buffalo Gap Wine & Food Summit.

While that may sound high-falutin', it doesn't interfere with people having a grand time when we convene each April for three days under tents and in our oak grove. Along with wine experts from around the world, we bring in guest chefs, including Texas legends Stephan Pyles and Jon Bonnell and internationally recognized celebrities such as Jacques Pépin and Francis Mallmann.

Preparing to serve 250 guests at "The Great American Steakhouse Experience" at the 2019 Buffalo Gap Wine & Food Summit.

The Perini Martini

SERVES 1

Blue cheese–stuffed olives

3 ounces Tito's Handmade Vodka

½ ounce olive brine

1 teaspoon dry vermouth

There aren't too many words that rhyme with Perini, so we couldn't resist this name for our classic martini, shaken and "dirty." It's made with Tito's Handmade vodka from Austin. Corn based, rather than wheat or potato, it has a sweeter edge and mellow character, perfect for sipping. At one time, we garnished the martini with green olives stuffed with jalapeños, but at the Steakhouse we now use olives hand-filled with blue cheese.

1. Skewer one or two olives on a mini bamboo skewer or toothpick. Fill a martini glass with ice and a little water to chill it.

2. Place the vodka, olive brine, vermouth, and a handful of ice in a cocktail shaker. Cover and shake the hell out of it for at least 20 seconds. You want the shaker to become so cold you can barely hold it. Discard the ice and water from the martini glass, then immediately strain the martini into the glass and garnish with the skewered olives. Serve immediately.

TEXAS VODKA

In 1995, Bert "Tito" Beveridge opened the first Texas distillery since Prohibition when he started Tito's Handmade in an Austin shack. Tito's is now one of the best-selling vodkas in America and is widely available internationally. Tito continues to make the vodka in pot stills he designed after researching historic photos of pre-Prohibition distilling. Each and every batch continues to be taste-tested for consistency. As the leading force behind the Texas crafts spirit industry, he even helped rewrite state laws for distilling spirits, opening the way for the numerous other Texas distilleries of vodka, whiskey, and gin that have popped up like bluebonnets in the spring.

Tito's previous work as a geologist also helped him figure out the process for making quality vodka. His vodka is distilled with spring water that has run over our state's abundant limestone, making it much more nuanced than many mass-produced spirits. Deep Eddy and other Texas vodka producers have followed his lead. Look for these spirits to make fine cocktails or just for sipping on the rocks.

Old-Fashioned

SERVES 1

1 teaspoon Demerara sugar or other raw sugar

2 dashes Angostura bitters

2 dashes orange bitters

2 ounces Maker's Mark or other bourbon

½ teaspoon juice from a jar of Luxardo cherries

Strip of orange peel

1 or 2 Luxardo cherries

The old-fashioned is so iconic that the glass for it—as well as for numerous other cocktails—is known as an old-fashioned glass. We have a special fondness for this smooth bourbon-based drink because it was a favorite of Tom's grandfather Frank.

1. Muddle the sugar with the bitters and a splash of the bourbon in the bottom of an old-fashioned glass. Fill glass three-quarters full of ice. Pour in the cherry juice and remaining bourbon and stir.

2. Rub the orange peel around the rim of the glass, add it to the top of the drink along with the cherry (or cherries), and serve.

Stan's Magic Coffee

SERVES 1

1 ounce hot espresso

1 ounce Bailey's Irish Cream Liqueur

1 ounce amaretto or Disaronno Originale

Whipped cream

Ground cinnamon

Stan Smith was a beloved longtime manager of the Steakhouse. This coffee drink was a favorite of his, whenever a "blue norther" cold front sent temperatures plummeting. It's perfectly celebratory too, around the holidays.

1. In a mug, stir together the espresso, Bailey's, and amaretto. Top with a spoonful of whipped cream, sprinkle with cinnamon, and serve right away.

OLD-FASHIONED

SALADS & SOUPS

When the Steakhouse opened, we offered one salad—greens with ranch dressing. Our world of salads has expanded quite a bit since those early days, with more greens, beans, corn, and even watermelon with a jalapeño vinaigrette. We've also added a few soups and stews to our repertoire, which are always welcome when there's a little nip in the air. All are tasty ways to start a meal.

The Ranch Salad

SERVES 6

BUTTERMILK RANCH DRESSING

½ cup buttermilk

½ cup mayonnaise

Half of a 0.4-ounce packet Hidden Valley Original Ranch seasoning

SALAD

3 cups torn green-leaf lettuce

3 cups torn romaine leaves

3 cups torn iceberg lettuce leaves

18 cherry tomatoes

½ heaping cup thinly sliced button mushrooms

½ small red onion, thinly sliced into half-moons and separated

Freshly ground black pepper, optional

When Tom opened the Steakhouse, there was one salad on the menu, and this was it! He wasn't a big fan of making too many decisions during dinner, so this one salad, served with only ranch dressing, was his solution.

Ranch dressing is arguably America's favorite condiment, and it's certainly the country's top-selling salad dressing. Nowhere is ranch dressing more beloved than here in Texas, where "buttermilk dressing" dates back as far as the 1930s, when it was documented in a San Antonio newspaper. A decade later, the folks behind the Hidden Valley Ranch in California popularized a similar dressing. We like that version so much that it tops our classic tossed salad, which is served with the majority of our entrees.

1. **To Make the Dressing:** Combine the buttermilk, mayonnaise, and seasoning in a jar. Cover and shake vigorously to combine. Refrigerate for 30 minutes. (Shake again before using.) Makes 1 cup. (Any leftover dressing will keep refrigerated for at least a few days.)

2. **To Assemble the Salad:** Combine all the greens in a large salad bowl. Top with the tomatoes, mushrooms, and red onion. Give the dressing another shake, then dress the salad to taste. Serve from the bowl or arrange equal portions on individual salad plates. In either case, offer the pepper mill and serve.

RANCH DRESSING

We overheard someone recently declare that ranch dressing was just gravy for salad. The Association for Dressings and Sauces—yes, there's really an industry trade group called that—says that 40 percent of Americans claim ranch as their favorite salad topping. The next closest is Italian dressing, at a contrastingly puny 10 percent. From further online reports, the average American eats ranch dressing 15 times a year. Lisa thinks, though, that there are Texans who eat it 15 times a day. She's partial to it herself, with potato chips. Not long ago, we were asked about providing a ranch dressing fountain for a wedding. One of our employee's sons used to beg to drink it by the glass. Neither of these last things happened, but you start to see a pattern here!

Wedge Salad with Blue Cheese Dressing

SERVES 4 OR MORE

BLUE CHEESE DRESSING

1 cup mayonnaise

¼ cup buttermilk

¼ cup sour cream

¼ cup plus 2 tablespoons extra virgin olive oil

¼ cup white wine vinegar

1½ teaspoons minced garlic

¼ teaspoon freshly ground black pepper

2 cups Danish blue cheese crumbles

SALAD

4 thick slices bacon

8 cups chopped romaine or a combination of romaine and

iceberg lettuce

2 Roma tomatoes, chopped

½ cup Danish blue cheese crumbles

Freshly ground black pepper

Crisp and cool, our wedge is almost as popular as our ranch salad. Many of our customers tell us that they don't like blue cheese, until they try this salad. We use Danish blue cheese, which has a mild, sweet quality. And of course, the inclusion of bacon makes everything taste better. The dressing also makes a great dip for tortilla chips, spicy chicken wings, and Fried Quail Legs (page 82).

1. **To Make the Dressing:** Whisk together the mayonnaise, buttermilk, sour cream, olive oil, vinegar, garlic, and pepper in a bowl. Stir in the blue cheese. Makes about 3 cups. Refrigerate until needed, or up to several days.

2. **To Make the Salad:** Put the bacon slices in a cold skillet. Turn the heat to medium-low and cook the bacon for 3 minutes on one side. Turn the bacon and cook on the other side to desired doneness. Remove the bacon with a slotted spoon and drain on paper towels. When cool enough to handle, crumble the bacon with your fingers and set aside.

Just before serving, cut the cold lettuce through its stem end into 4 or 6 wedges. Remove any loose, limp leaves and discard them. Arrange the wedges on well-chilled salad plates, spoon the dressing over each, and sprinkle equally with bacon, tomatoes, blue cheese, and a good grinding of black pepper. Serve immediately.

Corn and Shishito Salad

SERVES 4 TO 6

CUMIN VINAIGRETTE

3 tablespoons extra virgin olive oil

2 tablespoons fresh lime juice

¾ teaspoon kosher salt

¼ teaspoon ground cumin

⅓ cup diced red onion

1 garlic clove, minced

SALAD

2 tablespoons extra virgin olive oil

6 ounces shishito peppers, cut crosswise into ¼-inch slices, or 1 small green bell pepper, minced

1 large fresh jalapeño, minced

3 cups fresh corn kernels (from 5 to 6 ears of corn)

1 teaspoon kosher salt, or more to taste

⅓ cup crumbled feta cheese

Approximately ¼ cup chopped fresh cilantro leaves

All chiles came initially from the New World, but given how tasty they are, it's not surprising that they've circled the globe. The shishito, a small, thin-walled pepper that was bred in Japan, arrived in the Americas a couple of decades ago and has since created quite the sensation. The heat level is way below that Texas fave, the jalapeño, part of its broad appeal. Find them at farmers markets and well-stocked supermarkets from spring through fall. The little green chile pods pair beautifully with corn for this summery salad. For a heartier salad, mix in a couple of slices of crumbled crisp-cooked bacon, when you add the cilantro at the end.

1. **To Make the Vinaigrette:** Whisk together the oil, lime juice, salt, and cumin in a small bowl. Mix in the onion and garlic and let the mixture stand for about 10 minutes. (This helps the raw onion mellow a bit.)

2. **To Make the Salad:** Warm the oil in a medium skillet over medium heat. Add the shishitos and jalapeño and sauté for 1 minute, just to soften the peppers. Add the corn and salt and sauté for about 3 minutes more, long enough to take the raw edge off the corn. Spoon the corn mixture into a serving bowl and toss it with the vinaigrette. Cool briefly and mix in the cheese. Taste and add a bit more salt if needed. Refrigerate for at least 30 minutes. Stir in the cilantro just before serving.

Black Bean and Roasted Corn Salad

SERVES 8

VINAIGRETTE

⅔ cup vegetable oil

2 tablespoons white or apple cider vinegar

½ teaspoon Dijon mustard

½ teaspoon kosher salt

½ teaspoon freshly ground black pepper

SALAD

Two 15.5-ounce cans black beans, rinsed and drained

3 ears roasted or otherwise cooked corn on the cob, kernels sliced off

1 red bell pepper, seeded and diced

1 cup thinly sliced green onions

2 garlic cloves, minced

1 tablespoon minced fresh cilantro leaves

When you need a salad that won't wilt in a steamy Texas July, this one is always a good bet. It can also be served as salsa with tortillas or chips, or as an eye-catching topper for grilled chicken breasts. At the Steakhouse, we grill-roast in-season fresh ears of corn, then cut off the kernels and freeze them for use throughout the year.

1. To Make the Vinaigrette: Combine the oil, vinegar, mustard, salt, and pepper in a bowl. Whisk until well combined. Makes about ¾ cup.

2. To Assemble the Salad: Lightly toss the beans and corn together in a serving bowl. Stir in about three-quarters of the dressing along with the bell pepper, green onions, garlic, and cilantro. Taste and add additional dressing, if desired. Refrigerate the salad for at least 30 minutes. Stir again before serving.

Creamy Jalapeño Coleslaw

SERVES 6

4 cups shredded green cabbage

4 cups shredded red cabbage

½ cup Italian salad dressing, such as Wish-Bone

½ cup Buttermilk Ranch Dressing (page 100)

¼ cup brine from a jar of pickled jalapeños, or more to taste

Kosher salt

Here's another one of those recipes that's more than the sum of its parts. Our late friend and well-known Tex-Mex restaurateur, Matt Martinez, came up with this tangy combo. Matt and his family have been in the restaurant business in Austin and Dallas for decades, and Matt's charm and colorful personality were a force of nature.

1. Combine the green cabbage, red cabbage, Italian dressing, and ranch dressing in a bowl. Toss well. Add the jalapeño liquid. Taste and add salt, and more jalapeño liquid for more tang and heat. Cover and refrigerate for 30 minutes, or up to several hours. Serve chilled.

Cucumber-Sweet Onion Salad

SERVES 8

2 pounds unpeeled cucumbers, sliced ¼ inch thick

1 large Texas 1015 onion or other sweet onion, sliced ¼ inch thick

2 cups white vinegar

1½ cups granulated sugar

2 tablespoons black peppercorns

2 teaspoons kosher salt

1 to 2 tablespoons chopped fresh parsley, cilantro, or a combination, optional

Dr. Leonard Pike of Texas A&M's famous agricultural school spent years perfecting a sweet, rather than tear-inducing, onion that would grow well in Texas. Called the Texas 1015, because October 15 is the optimum planting date, this super-sweet onion has been the Texas state vegetable since 1997. Use a true sweet onion—a Texas 1015, Vidalia, or Maui. The characteristic they share is a low level of pyruvate, the naturally occurring chemical compound in onions that makes you weep. That makes the onions a perfect mate for cucumbers in this quick pickled salad. Let the vegetables soak up the tangy liquid for at least a few hours, or up to 24 hours if you have the time.

1. Place the cucumbers and onions in a heatproof bowl. Combine 1 cup water with the vinegar, sugar, peppercorns, salt, and herbs (if using) in a saucepan. Bring to a boil and pour over the cucumbers and onions. Stir well. Cool to room temperature. Cover and refrigerate for at least 4 hours or up to 24 hours, then use a slotted spoon to serve.

CREAMY JALAPEÑO COLESLAW

SEE PAGE 106

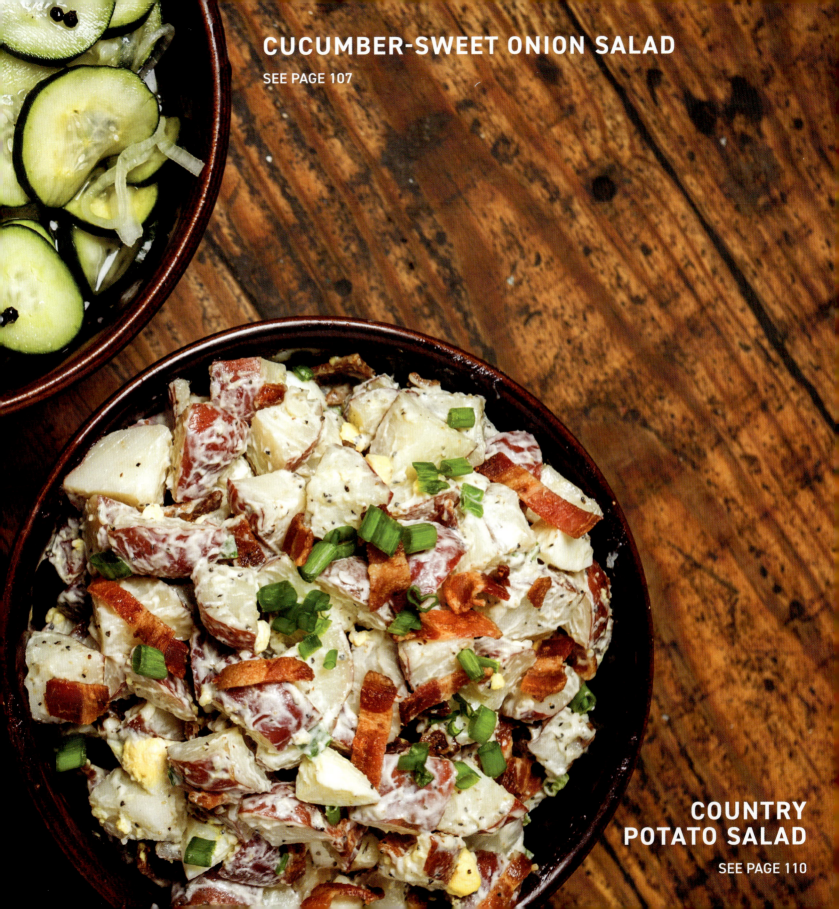

CUCUMBER-SWEET ONION SALAD

SEE PAGE 107

COUNTRY POTATO SALAD

SEE PAGE 110

Country Potato Salad

SERVES 8

POTATO SALAD

6 slices bacon

2½ to 3 pounds unpeeled red waxy potatoes, such as Red Bliss, cut into bite-size pieces

1 teaspoon kosher salt

2 hard-boiled eggs, chopped

2 green onions, thinly sliced

DRESSING

1 tablespoon bacon drippings

½ cup mayonnaise

2 teaspoons Dijon mustard

1 to 1½ teaspoons kosher salt

½ teaspoon freshly ground black pepper

Lisa says no one likes "gloppy"—whether it's coleslaw, potato salad, or any dish made with mayonnaise or other dressing. The key to great potato salad is to keep it simple and light. Start with a smaller amount of dressing; you can always add more. Thanks to our friend Matthew Wendel for his inspiration here. Matty, as he's known, is quite a chef, and we became fast friends while he worked for President George W. Bush and First Lady Laura Bush.

1. To Make the Salad: Put the bacon slices in a cold skillet. Turn the heat to medium-low and cook the bacon for 3 minutes on one side. Turn the bacon and cook on the other side to desired doneness. Remove the bacon with a slotted spoon and drain on paper towels. Carefully pour 1 table-spoon of the bacon drippings into a small dish and set aside for the dressing. When the bacon is cool enough to handle, crumble with your fingers and set aside.

Place the potatoes in a large saucepan and cover with cold water. Add the salt and bring to a boil over high heat. Reduce the heat to a simmer and cook until the potatoes are tender when pierced with a fork, 20 to 25 minutes. Drain the potatoes and transfer to a large bowl.

2. To Make the Dressing: Whisk together the reserved bacon drippings, mayonnaise, mustard, salt, and pepper in a medium bowl.

3. Pour the dressing over the potatoes and gently stir in the eggs and bacon. Cover with plastic wrap and refrigerate for a minimum of 2 hours, or up to overnight. Let the potato salad come to room temperature for 20 to 30 minutes. Stir in the green onions just before serving.

Texas Caviar

SERVES 8 TO 10

Two 15.5-ounce cans black-eyed peas, rinsed and drained

1 large tomato, diced

½ cup sliced green onions

½ cup diced red onion

1 jalapeño, seeded and finely diced

2 garlic cloves, minced

¾ cup vegetable oil

¼ cup white or apple cider vinegar

1 teaspoon minced fresh oregano leaves, or ½ teaspoon crumbled dried oregano

1 teaspoon minced fresh basil leaves, or ½ teaspoon dried basil

½ teaspoon kosher salt, or more to taste

½ teaspoon freshly ground black pepper, or more to taste

Lettuce leaves, for serving

This humble black-eyed pea salad with the name "caviar" appears on picnic tables, buffets, and at Sunday suppers throughout Texas.

1. Combine the black-eyed peas, tomato, green onions, red onion, jalapeño, and garlic in a bowl and mix. Add the oil, vinegar, oregano, basil, and salt and pepper and toss together. Cover and refrigerate for at least 6 hours, stirring occasionally.

2. Before serving, drain off any excess dressing and tuck a few lettuce leaves around the peas. Serve chilled or at room temperature.

Avocado-Grapefruit Salad with Poppy Seed Dressing

SERVES 6 TO 8

POPPY SEED DRESSING

¾ cup vegetable oil

¼ cup white or apple cider vinegar

½ cup granulated sugar

3 tablespoons poppy seeds

1 tablespoon Dijon mustard

½ teaspoon kosher salt

AVOCADO-GRAPEFRUIT SALAD

1 head romaine, torn into bite-size pieces

3 red grapefruits, preferably Ruby Sweet or Rio Star, peeled, membranes removed, and sectioned

2 large avocados, halved, pitted, and thinly sliced

1 small red onion, sliced into paper-thin rings

Before there were well-known Texas chefs like Stephan Pyles, Dean Fearing, and Robert Del Grande, there was Helen Corbitt. She was a chef and culinary pioneer who introduced mid-century Texas to finer foods and wine. In five cookbooks and her work at bastions like Austin's Driskill Hotel and the flagship Neiman Marcus in Dallas, she transformed Texas ingredients into dishes that are now considered classics. This combination of avocados and grapefruit sections with a dollop of a German-inspired sweet-and-sour poppy seed dressing was one of her many signature dishes. It remains a Texas favorite, and we've fine-tuned our own version. Look for Texas Ruby Sweet or Rio Star grapefruit for their superior color and sweetness from November to April.

1. **To Make the Dressing:** Combine the oil, vinegar, sugar, poppy seeds, mustard, and salt in a quart jar. Cover and shake vigorously to combine. Makes 1½ cups. (Leftover dressing can be refrigerated for 1 week.)

2. **To Assemble the Salad:** Toss the romaine with about one-quarter of the dressing and arrange in a bowl or on individual salad plates. Arrange the grapefruit and avocado slices neatly over the romaine, alternating colors. Scatter the onion slices over the top. Drizzle the salad with more dressing and serve.

Elegant Blue Cheese Potato Salad

SERVES 6 OR MORE

¼ cup (½ stick) unsalted butter

2 tablespoons bacon drippings, or additional unsalted butter

2½ pounds red waxy potatoes, unpeeled, cut into ½-inch pieces

1½ teaspoons fine sea salt

1½ teaspoons granulated garlic

¾ teaspoon ground black pepper

¾ cup Blue Cheese Dressing (page 102)

4 ounces blue cheese crumbles, preferably Danish or other mild blue cheese

½ pound bacon, chopped into 1-inch pieces, and cooked until crisp

2 green onions, sliced thin, both green and white portions

Every year, we cater the late summer gala at The Grace Museum in downtown Abilene. The event has no cooking facilities, so we have the fun challenge of figuring out suitable dishes to bring, already prepared and then held and served at room temperature. We created this sumptuous dish for those circumstances, but it's just as good freshly put together in your home kitchen.

1. Heat the oven to 325°F. Place the butter and bacon drippings in a pan and warm over medium heat until they have melted. Scatter the potatoes on a baking sheet or in a pan or dish large enough to hold them in a single layer. Drizzle with the butter mixture. Stir together the salt, garlic, and pepper and sprinkle over the potatoes. Toss the potatoes well to coat with the butter mixture and seasonings. Bake the potatoes for a total of 50 to 55 minutes, until tender, stirring after about 30 minutes.

2. Transfer the potatoes to a shallow serving dish. Toss with ½ cup of the blue cheese dressing and let sit at room temperature. Shortly before serving, toss potatoes with the remaining blue cheese dressing. Sprinkle with the blue cheese and bacon, then top with green onions. Serve at room temperature.

Layered Avocado Salad

SERVES 6 TO 8

¼ cup plus 2 tablespoons extra virgin olive oil

3 tablespoons red wine vinegar

¼ cup grated Parmesan and Romano cheese blend

1½ tablespoons Dijon mustard

¼ cup chopped green onions

2 garlic cloves, minced

1 teaspoon kosher salt

½ teaspoon freshly ground black pepper

2 large avocados, pitted, peeled, and cubed

1 large head romaine, cut into bite-size pieces, or one 9-ounce bag romaine leaves

When it's so hot in Texas that hens lay hard-boiled eggs, this salad is sure to cool you down. We appropriated the recipe from our friends Jon and Jackie Means while visiting their H-Y Ranch. The H-Y looks out over some of the most stunning landscape of the Gila Wilderness in Grant County, New Mexico.

Make the salad early in the day, pull it out of the refrigerator when you're ready to eat, and give it a toss. Add some cooked shrimp to turn it into a main course.

1. Combine the olive oil, vinegar, cheese, mustard, green onions, garlic, salt, and pepper in a shallow 8x10-inch serving dish. Using a fork, mix the dressing ingredients to blend well.

2. Add the avocado and stir gently to coat with the dressing. Arrange the romaine on top of the avocado, but do not toss. Cover with plastic wrap and refrigerate for 6 to 8 hours. Toss the salad just before serving.

Watermelon-Pecan Salad with Jalapeño Vinaigrette

SERVES 6

JALAPEÑO VINAIGRETTE

½ cup jalapeño jelly

¼ cup white vinegar

WATERMELON-PECAN SALAD

¾ cup coarsely chopped pecans

3 to 4 cups chopped arugula

5 heaping cups 1-inch-cubed watermelon

1 cup Danish blue cheese crumbles

Texas farmers produce more tons of luscious summer watermelons than those in almost every other state. In this cool, refreshing salad, tangy, slightly salty blue cheese pairs surprisingly well with the melon, pecans add crunch, and jalapeño jelly gives the whole dish a bit of sweet heat. Make the dressing and prep the other ingredients up to an hour before serving so the salad can be assembled at the last minute.

1. **To Make the Vinaigrette:** Combine the jelly and vinegar in a lidded jar. Cover and shake well.

2. **To Make the Salad:** Toast the pecans in a small skillet over medium heat until fragrant, about 5 minutes.

Arrange the arugula on a platter or individual salad plates. Divide the watermelon cubes over the arugula. Shake the dressing before spooning half of it on top of the arugula and watermelon. Top with the blue cheese crumbles and pecans. Serve, passing the remaining dressing at the table. Or, toss the arugula, watermelon, blue cheese, pecans, and dressing in a bowl.

Kale Salad

SERVES 4 TO 6

DRESSING

2 tablespoons white balsamic vinegar, or 1 tablespoon regular balsamic vinegar and 1 tablespoon rice vinegar

1 tablespoon rice vinegar

1 tablespoon honey

2 tablespoons extra virgin olive oil

½ teaspoon fine sea salt, or more to taste

SALAD

1 large bunch of kale, enough to yield about 8 loosely packed cups, tough ribs removed, chopped into bite-size pieces

¼ cup dried cranberries

¼ cup pine nuts, lightly toasted in a dry skillet

½ cup shaved Parmesan cheese

Freshly ground black pepper

Yes, indeed, cowboys have been known to eat kale, especially when it's gussied up with a sweet-and-sour dressing and garnished with buttery pine nuts, dried cranberries, and shavings of Parmesan cheese.

1. **To Make the Dressing:** At least 20 minutes before you want to assemble the salad, whisk together the ingredients in a large bowl.

2. **To Assemble the Salad:** Toss the kale together with the dressing and let sit at room temperature about 20 minutes. After about 10 minutes, give it another toss. The kale will soften and reduce by about one-third in volume. Mix in the dried cranberries. The salad can continue to sit at room temperature for another 30 minutes or so or be refrigerated for up to a couple of hours.

Shortly before serving, add the pine nuts and Parmesan to the salad, season with pepper, and serve.

Spanish Tomato Salad

SERVES 4 OR MORE

2 large (about 1 pound each) red-ripe beefsteak tomatoes

Coarse sea salt or kosher salt

Freshly ground black pepper

2 tablespoons best-quality extra virgin olive oil

1½ teaspoons sherry vinegar

1 teaspoon minced garlic

1 teaspoon crumbled dried oregano

2 tablespoons chopped fresh parsley

Really great summer beefsteak tomatoes don't need much to dress them up. This preparation enhances them a bit without overwhelming them.

1. Thinly slice the tomatoes, neatly cutting out any hard cores. Place the tomato slices on a baking sheet in a single layer. Season generously with salt and pepper and let sit for about 5 minutes.

2. Meanwhile, prepare the salad dressing, whisking together the oil and vinegar with the garlic and oregano in a small bowl. Season with a bit of salt and pepper.

Shake any watery liquid off the tomatoes and arrange them in a large, shallow bowl. Drizzle the dressing over the tomatoes and sprinkle the parsley over them. Serve at room temperature.

Zucchini "Carpaccio"

SERVES 6

2 medium zucchini

Kosher salt

Freshly ground black pepper

2 garlic cloves, thinly sliced

½ large lemon

3 tablespoons extra virgin olive oil

2 to 3 tablespoons pine nuts, toasted

1 tablespoon honey

1 chunk Parmesan cheese

¼ cup torn fresh mint leaves

The theme of the 2017 Buffalo Gap Wine & Food Summit was "Return to Our Roots." For the first time, we cooked Italian food for 200-plus guests to celebrate the Swiss-Italian heritage of the Perini family. Thinly sliced zucchini—use a mandoline—with pine nuts, Parmesan shavings, and some top-notch olive oil are combined in this bright salad.

1. Using a mandoline, slice the zucchini lengthwise as thinly as possible. Place the zucchini ribbons in a colander, sprinkle well with salt, and place the colander over a plate. Let the zucchini drain, tossing occasionally, for about 30 minutes. Transfer the zucchini to paper towels and pat dry.

2. Arrange the zucchini in a shallow baking dish in several layers, tucking garlic slices between the ribbons. Squeeze the lemon over the zucchini, cover, and refrigerate for at least 15 minutes, or up to a couple of hours.

3. When ready to serve, arrange the zucchini on individual plates, decoratively curling or swirling up some of the ribbons. Drizzle with the olive oil and scatter on the pine nuts. Add a few dots of honey to each plate, then shave Parmesan over each, garnish with the mint, sprinkle with salt and pepper, and serve.

Wild Rice Salad

SERVES 6 TO 8

1 quart (4 cups) low-sodium chicken stock

1 teaspoon kosher salt

1 cup wild rice

2 tablespoons extra virgin olive oil

1½ tablespoons fruity balsamic vinegar, preferably raspberry

1 teaspoon granulated sugar

½ teaspoon ground black pepper

½ cup seedless green grapes, halved

½ cup pecan pieces, toasted

⅓ cup dried cranberries

2 medium green onions, both white and green portions, sliced thinly

Here's a dramatic looking salad, featuring charcoal-colored rice dotted with bright bits of red and green. Pecans enhance the nuttiness of the rice. Just a bit of dressing pulls it all together. It's good for a buffet because it can sit a while at room temperature without losing any of its pizzazz.

1. Combine the stock and salt in a large saucepan and bring to a boil over high heat. Stir in wild rice, cover, and reduce heat to a low simmer. Cook rice until quite tender with some grains bursting, 45 to 50 minutes. Remove from heat and let wild rice sit covered for 10 to 15 minutes. Drain off any excess liquid.

2. Scrape the wild rice into a large bowl. Mix together the oil, vinegar, sugar, and pepper in a separate bowl. Pour over the wild rice and toss together well. Mix in the grapes, pecans, cranberries, and green onions. Let sit at room temperature for 30 minutes for the flavors to meld. Serve at room temperature or refrigerate for later use.

Wedding Pasta Salad

SERVES 6

Kosher salt

8 ounces bowtie pasta

DRESSING

2 tablespoons extra virgin olive oil

1 medium shallot, minced

1 teaspoon minced garlic

2 tablespoons fresh lemon juice

¼ cup grated Parmesan cheese

Kosher salt and freshly ground black pepper

VEGETABLES

1 tablespoon extra virgin olive oil

½ cup diced yellow bell pepper

½ cup diced red bell pepper

½ cup diced orange bell pepper

½ cup diced red onion

3 cups packed chopped spinach leaves

1 heaping cup halved grape tomatoes

One 8-ounce jar sliced sun-dried tomatoes in oil, not drained

2 tablespoons grated Parmesan cheese

We were working on the wedding plans for family friends—the Kinards in Abilene—when Terri (mom of the bride) shared this flavorful and colorful pasta salad recipe. It's been served at many weddings since, and we appreciate the recipe!

1. Bring a large pot of water to a boil and add 1 tablespoon salt. Add the bowties and cook, stirring occasionally, until tender but still firm to the bite. Drain the bowties in a colander.

2. To Make the Dressing: Combine the oil, shallot, and garlic in a bowl and let sit for 15 minutes. Whisk in the lemon juice, Parmesan, and a couple of pinches of salt and pepper.

3. To Cook the Vegetables: Warm the oil in a skillet over medium heat. Add the bell peppers and red onion and sauté for 2 to 3 minutes, just until the vegetables lose their raw flavor. Stir in the spinach and grape tomatoes and remove from the heat. Add the sun-dried tomatoes and their oil to the mixture. Spoon into a large shallow bowl.

4. Spoon the hot pasta over the vegetables and toss to combine. Add the dressing and toss again. Scatter the 2 tablespoons Parmesan over the salad. Cover and refrigerate for at least 1 hour, or up to overnight. Bring back to room temperature before serving.

SERVES 6

BACON VINAIGRETTE

4 slices bacon

1 tablespoon all-purpose flour

½ cup warm water

½ cup white or apple cider vinegar

2 tablespoons granulated sugar

½ teaspoon dried oregano

Kosher salt and freshly ground black pepper

SIRLOIN SALAD

One 1- to 1¼-pound top sirloin steak, 1 inch thick

½ teaspoon kosher salt

1 teaspoon freshly ground black pepper

1 red bell pepper, halved and seeded

1 white onion, sliced into thick rounds

2 medium heads romaine, cut into thin ribbons

1 tablespoon minced fresh flat-leaf parsley leaves

1 tablespoon minced fresh basil leaves

Chuck Wagon Sirloin Salad with Bacon Vinaigrette

This main dish salad sprang from our work with the Texas Beef Council. With the council, we have had the good fortune to visit many countries around the globe that import US beef—Poland, Russia, Japan, Mexico, Dominican Republic, and Bermuda. We've made appearances on local TV shows, at newspaper offices, and special events, such as parties at the residences of American ambassadors in some of these countries. The salad is a great way to use any leftover steak, from sirloin to flank to flat-iron to ribeye.

1. **To Make the Vinaigrette:** Put the bacon slices in a cold skillet. Turn the heat to medium-low and cook the bacon for 3 minutes on one side. Turn the bacon and cook on the other side to desired doneness. Remove the bacon with a slotted spoon and drain on paper towels. Reserve the drippings in the skillet and turn the heat up to medium. Add the flour to the drippings and cook, stirring continuously, until dissolved. Continuing to stir, add the warm water, vinegar, and sugar and cook until thickened. Add the oregano and salt and pepper to taste and set aside. When the bacon slices are cool enough to handle, cut them up into small pieces and set aside.

2. **To Grill the Steak:** Fire up the grill for a two-level fire capable of cooking at the same time on both high heat (1 to 2 seconds with the hand test—page 147) and medium heat (4 to 5 seconds with the hand test). If grilling over gas or charcoal, add a half-dozen mesquite chunks to the fire shortly before placing the steak on the grill. Season the steak with the salt and pepper. Grill the steak uncovered over high heat for 2½ to 3 minutes per side. Move the steak to medium heat, turning again, and continue grilling for 2½ to 3 minutes per side for medium-rare (a total of 10 to 12 minutes). The steak should be turned a minimum of three times, more often if juices begin to pool on top.

3. At the same time, grill the bell pepper and onion uncovered over medium heat, turning them at least once, until tender. Plan on 8 to 10 minutes for the bell pepper and 14 to 16 minutes for the onion slices.

4. When the pepper is cool enough to handle, remove any loose charred skin and slice the pepper into thin ribbons. Slice the meat diagonally across the grain into ¼-inch-thick strips. Save any juices from the meat and vegetables and add them to the dressing.

5. **To Assemble the Salad:** Make a bed of romaine, parsley, and basil on a platter or on individual dinner plates. Arrange the steak, bell pepper, and onion slices over the greens. Drizzle with the warm dressing, scatter the bacon pieces, and serve.

Fajita Salad

SERVES 4

CHIPOTLE RANCH DRESSING

1 cup Buttermilk Ranch Dressing (page 100)

1 to 2 chipotles from a can of chipotles in adobo

STEAK

One 1½-pound skirt steak, trimmed of membranes and excess fat

¼ cup Perini Ranch Steak Rub

2 limes, halved

SALAD

Approximately 8 cups torn or sliced romaine or iceberg lettuce

1 heaping cup chopped ripe red tomatoes

1 cup canned black beans, rinsed and drained

1 avocado, peeled, pitted, and cut in thin, lengthwise slices

Approximately 12 Tortilla Chips (page 62)

8 ounces (about 2 cups) crumbled cotija cheese or queso fresco

This just bursts with Southwestern flavor. It's more of an assembly of building blocks that we always have on hand, but not too complicated to make from scratch when you're in the mood. We use Nolan Ryan's skirt steak for this. You may know him better as a baseball player, but he's been raising cattle, mostly Angus, in Texas for more than 40 years. If you don't have our ranch Steak Rub, just salt and pepper the meat well before grilling. Have all the ingredients ready before you head to the grill, so that you can add warm juicy slices of the fajita steak to the cool greens and other ingredients.

1. To Make the Dressing: Puree the ranch dressing and chipotle chiles in a blender or food processor. This is a fairly small amount for either appliance, so you may have to stop and scrape down the sides a time or two. Refrigerate until needed.

2. To Prepare the Steak: Cut the steak in half to make two shorter, more manageable pieces. Massage the skirt steak with the dry rub. Let the steak sit uncovered at room temperature while preparing the grill.

Fire up the grill for a two-level fire capable of cooking first on high heat (1 to 2 seconds with the hand test—see page 147) and then on medium (4 to 5 seconds with the hand test). If grilling over gas or charcoal, add a half-dozen mesquite chunks to the fire shortly before placing the steak on the grill.

Grill the steaks over high heat for about 2 minutes per side if less than ½ inch thick, or 3 to 4 minutes per side if more than ½ inch thick. Place the lime halves over medium heat. Grill them just until they heat through and develop a few brown spots. Move the steaks to medium heat and cook another couple of minutes on each side, until medium-rare. Turn the steaks more often if juice pools on the surface. Tent with aluminum foil and let rest for 5 minutes.

3. While the meat sits, arrange the salad greens on 4 plates, dividing them equally. Drizzle each with chipotle ranch dressing. Add the other salad ingredients to each plate, arranging them neatly.

4. Cut the steak. Holding a knife at a slight diagonal, slice the steaks across the grain into thin, finger-length strips. Arrange a portion of steak over the other salad ingredients. Top each portion with some of the cheese and serve.

TOM'S TIP: You might find something labeled chicken or shrimp fajitas, but the Spanish term really refers to skirt steak, a long flat cut that comes from under the rib cage. While it's known for its beefy flavor and juiciness, it can be tough if not cut properly. Make sure to slice it against the grain and slightly on the diagonal, or else you'll end up with stringy pieces more akin to boot leather. If buying your meat from a butcher, ask if the shop has "inside" skirt, which will be a bit more tender.

Cream of Mushroom Soup

SERVES 6 OR MORE

6 tablespoons (¾ stick) salted butter

1 tablespoon minced onion

½ pound mushrooms, chopped fine

4 cups low-sodium chicken stock

½ cup all-purpose flour

1 teaspoon table salt

1 cup heavy cream

2 tablespoons dry sherry

Crème fraîche or unsweetened whipped cream, optional

If you've only had the canned version of mushroom soup, this will be a revelation. It's the real deal, a recipe from one of our dearest friends, the late Bunny Becker. With husband Richard, Bunny founded Becker Vineyards some 30 years ago, and helped turn it into one of the most lauded wineries in Texas. Bunny was an excellent French-style cook, and we were lucky to enjoy many of her dishes. This relies on the French preparation called *duxelles*, where a mince of mushrooms with onion is cooked down to a rich paste, often with some cream and sherry. Oh my. While cups of the soup make an elegant start to a meal, steaming bowls of it, accompanied by a baguette and great red wine, make one of our favorite winter meals served by the fire.

1. Melt 2 tablespoons of the butter in a skillet over medium heat. Stir in the onion and sauté about 1 minute, until softened. Stir in the mushrooms and let the mixture cook for another 5 minutes, until they release their liquid. Pour in the stock, cover, and simmer for 15 minutes.

2. While the soup is simmering, melt the remaining butter in a medium saucepan over medium heat. Add the flour and salt and cook, stirring continually, until bubbly and thickened lightly, and the raw flour taste is eliminated, another few minutes. Scrape the mushroom mixture into the saucepan and pour in the cream. Stir and heat the soup through. In the last couple of minutes, add the sherry.

3. Ladle into cups or bowls and serve, topped with spoonfuls of crème fraîche or whipped cream if you wish.

TOM'S TIP: The soup freezes well, so you might want to make a double batch to have it on hand for another meal.

BECKER VINEYARDS

Dr. Richard Becker and his late wife, Bunny, partnered with Fess Parker and the two of us to create the Buffalo Gap Wine & Food Summit back in 2005. The Beckers had already been in the business of making Texas wine for a decade at their Becker Vineyards in Stonewall, outside of Fredericksburg. In fact, they were pioneers in the making of fine Texas wine, which was a tough sell in the early days. Bunny would load her dolly with cases of wine and cart them around from restaurant to restaurant, persistent but charming, imploring them to carry Becker wines. It worked. Their wines now can be found in noted dining establishments in Texas and across the country. They have been served on multiple occasions at the White House, the James Beard House, and the Texas Governor's Mansion. Today the winery cultivates approximately 66 acres of estate fruit, featuring 11 wine grapes. They also purchase premium grapes from a dozen grape growers in other parts of Texas. Just as we think it's worth going out of your way to come to our Steakhouse, it's well worth a detour to visit this beautiful Old World–style winery. It features an 1890s homestead log cabin and a reproduction of a 19th-century German stone barn, surrounded by lavender fields and wildflowers. You will always find a selection of Becker Vineyards wines on our Steakhouse wine list.

Butternut Squash Soup

**SERVES 8 IN BOWLS OR
MAKES SEVERAL DOZEN
SHOOTERS**

Vegetable oil spray

One 3-pound butternut squash, halved from the top down, seeds and guts scooped out

1 large onion, halved from the top down

2 tablespoons unsalted butter

3 cups low-sodium chicken stock

1 tablespoon granulated sugar

½ teaspoon ground ginger

½ teaspoon ground nutmeg

¼ teaspoon ground turmeric

¾ teaspoon table salt, or to taste

1 cup heavy cream

This is really popular at our catered events, especially served as individual shooters. Served in bowls, you might want to top it with a few toasted pepitas, or croutons, or a slight dusting of cayenne. It freezes and reheats well.

1. Heat the oven to 350°F. Mist a baking dish or roasting pan large enough to hold the two squash halves with vegetable oil spray. Arrange the squash, cut side up, and the onion halves in the dish. Add 1 tablespoon of butter to each squash cavity. Pour ¼ cup water around the squash and cover with foil. Bake about 1½ hours, until squash is very tender.

2. Let squash and onion sit in the baking dish, uncovered, until cool enough to handle. Scoop the squash pulp out of its skin and transfer it to a blender, with any melted butter or squash juices. Plop those onion halves in the blender too. Pour in the stock and add the sugar, spices, and salt. Puree the mixture. Pour the soup into a saucepan and stir in the cream. Warm the soup over medium-low heat for 10 to 15 minutes for the flavors to blend. Serve hot.

Green Chile Stew

SERVES 8

1¾ to 2 pounds beef chuck, cut in
½-inch cubes

2 medium onions, diced

4 garlic cloves, minced

1 to 1¼ pounds red potatoes,
peeled or unpeeled and diced

5 cups low-sodium beef or chicken
stock

1½ tablespoons table salt, or to
taste

3 cups chopped roasted New
Mexico green chiles, fresh or
thawed if frozen

1 cup corn kernels, fresh or frozen,
1 cup carrot chunks, or 1 diced red
bell pepper (or a combination of
these), optional

A bowl of comfort, this green chile stew comes from our friend and
co-author Cheryl Alters Jamison. Like most stews, it improves with a
night in the fridge before serving. Accompany with a stack of warm flour
tortillas or squares of cornbread.

1. Sear the meat in a Dutch oven or large heavy saucepan over medium-
high heat until it browns and the liquid accumulated from the meat mostly
evaporates. Stir in the onions and garlic and cook for several minutes, until
the onions become translucent. Add the potatoes and stock and scrape the
mixture up from the bottom to loosen the browned bits. Sprinkle in the
salt, reduce the heat to a low simmer, and cook uncovered for 1¼ hours.

2. Stir in the chiles and any or all of the optional ingredients and continue
cooking for another 45 minutes to 1 hour, until the meat is quite tender,
the vegetables are soft, and the flavors have blended together.

3. Ladle into bowls and serve hot.

BUTTERNUT SQUASH SOUP

SEE PAGE 132

BEEF

This is where it all began—Perini beef with a big helping of Perini hospitality. From the time that a teenaged Tom first took his Abilene high school buddies out to the family ranch to play cards, and maybe drink a few adult beverages, he grilled burgers for everyone. Since he opened the restaurant in 1983, beef has remained at the center of the plate. Whether wood-grilled steaks, smoked tenderloins or briskets, the best burgers, or slow-simmered chilis, we strive to serve meat of the highest quality. Our partnerships and friendships with Certified Angus Beef ™, Texas Beef Council, and Texas & Southwestern Cattle Raisers Association have helped us achieve this goal year after year. Now this is some good eating!

Cowboy Ribeye Steaks

SERVES 6 OR MORE

STEAK RUB

3 tablespoons kosher salt

1¾ teaspoons coarsely ground black pepper

½ teaspoon granulated garlic

½ teaspoon dried oregano

¼ teaspoon granulated onion

¼ teaspoon beef bouillon powder

Pinch of ground white pepper

Six 1- to 1¼-pound bone-in ribeye steaks, each 1½ inches thick

Steaks are celebration fare—for that big raise, a new addition to the family, or just making it through the week to another Friday night. Has any boss ever said, "You've done a great job on this project, let me take you out for a chicken breast"? Nope. Nothing quite satisfies the appetite like a beef steak, especially here in Texas. There's just nothing better than the richness and deep flavor of a well-marbled, bone-in ribeye, at least in Tom's opinion. Cut from the primal rib, the bone-in ribeye is the king of grilling steaks, known for its juiciness and flavor, more than earning its reputation as the connoisseur's cut. We were both particularly proud that *Texas Monthly* magazine, in its 2010 bucket list of 63 things to do in Texas before you die, implored its readers to visit the Perini Ranch Steakhouse and eat our ribeye steak. ("For a steak that tastes the way God intended, there's not a better place in Texas.") We were right up there with buying a pair of custom cowboy boots.

So, can you substitute boneless steaks? Yes, but the hefty bone contributes a significant amount of flavor. Tom says the difference between a nice restaurant and a joint is that at a joint you can pick up the bone and chew on it. Perini Ranch Steakhouse is definitely a joint.

1. Combine all the rub ingredients in a small bowl. Using your hands, coat the steaks all over with the rub. Pack it on well. Let the steaks sit at room temperature for about 30 minutes.

2. Fire up the grill for a two-level fire capable of cooking first on high heat (1 to 2 seconds with the hand test—see page 147) and then on medium (4 to 5 seconds with the hand test).

3. If grilling over gas or charcoal, add a half-dozen mesquite chunks to the fire shortly before placing the steaks on the grill. Grill the steaks over high heat for 2½ minutes per side. Move the steaks to medium heat, turning them again, and continue grilling for 2½ to 3 minutes per side for medium-rare. If meat juices begin to pool on the surface, turn more frequently. Serve immediately.

TOM'S TIP: The Spinalis dorsi—the extra-tender ribeye cap—is worth a splurge all by itself, if you can find it. While ribeye is considered the king of steaks, the cap is the jewel in its crown. It's the super-marbled, almost spongy muscle that curves around the outer rim of the prime rib. You or your butcher can trim it from the bigger cut if you wish. You want it to be at least ½ inch thick. Sometimes ribeye cap is rolled pinwheel-style and tied into something like filet medallions, but we like it grilled flat to get more of the contrast between the seared surface and the rare interior meat. Prepare it like the ribeye steak, grilling about 7 to 10 minutes total.

OUR BEEF BELIEF

Our friend, the cowboy poet and entertainer Red Steagall has a fabulous saying, "Every once in a while, in your life, you might need a doctor or a lawyer, but three times a day, seven days a week, you need a farmer or a rancher." Our commitment to beef, agriculture, ranching, and rural living runs deep, and we are honored to be a part of these industries. With Tom's ranching experience and Lisa's dairy farm South Carolina Lowcountry roots, it's only natural that we are dedicated to this lifestyle. It's not just a career, it's our life, and the heritage of West Texas on a plate.

GRAIN FED OR GRASS FED?

All cattle are grass fed at some point in their lives. Beef that has *only* been fed grass will usually be labelled as "grass finished" or "100% grass fed." Both grain and grass fed and finished are high in iron, zinc, and vitamin B12. Grass-finished beef has a lower carbon footprint, and a gamier, sharper flavor. Grain-finished beef is usually fed a blend of corn, oats, and barley. Grain-finished beef develops more marbling, or intramuscular fat, resulting in a smooth, almost buttery, and beefy flavor.

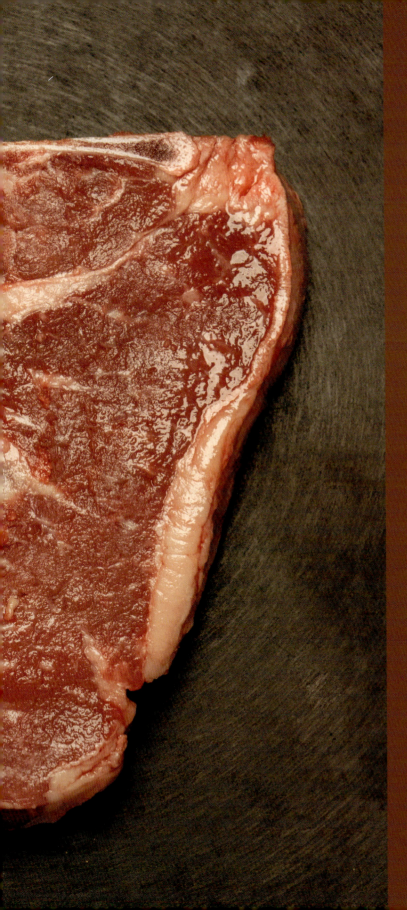

BUYING QUALITY BEEF

We serve Certified Angus Beef at the Steakhouse. The American Angus Association created the trademarked Certified Angus Beef program in cooperation with the USDA to help market its beef. Beef labeled CAB is a bit pricier, but gives the buyer assurance that the meat has been selected for meeting ten specifications of consistency in marbling and tenderness, which contribute to flavor. Only about 25 percent of Angus cattle raised in the U.S. qualify to be a part of this program. Look for CAB at your supermarket or butcher shop. The beef we use is grain finished, meaning that the cattle started their lives eating grass, but were later fed a diet of corn, sorghum, and other grains, which gives the meat a sweeter finish and more even marbling.

GRADE SCHOOLING

You've likely heard about grades of beef, particularly Prime and Choice, the top two specifications. USDA inspectors grade beef on characteristics such as marbling (the interior distribution of fat) to indicate its flavor, juiciness, and tenderness. Grading is a voluntary program, done at the behest of the meat packer, and typically requested for meat expected to be Prime or Choice. Very little meat makes Prime grade, and what does is mostly sold to restaurants, though quality meat markets today typically have a few Prime cuts. If you can, buy Certified Angus Beef which will be graded Choice or Prime. Otherwise, choose steaks that have fine, smooth intramuscular fat marbling. You'll be rewarded with great eating.

Strip Steaks

SERVES 6 OR MORE

STEAK RUB

¼ cup kosher salt

2 teaspoons coarsely ground black pepper

¾ teaspoon granulated garlic

¾ teaspoon ground oregano

¼ teaspoon granulated onion

¼ teaspoon beef bouillon powder

⅛ teaspoon ground white pepper

Six 14- to 16-ounce boneless strip steaks, each 1½ inches thick

Well-marbled strip steaks from the loin may be called New York, Kansas City, or even Delmonico strips. No matter the name, they all come from just behind the rib. A strip steak isn't as densely marbled as a ribeye or as tender as a filet. However, it has a beefier flavor than both. Make friends with your butcher and ask for steaks from the center of the loin.

1. Combine all the rub ingredients in a small bowl. Massage each steak generously with the dry rub. Let the steaks sit at room temperature for 30 minutes.

2. Fire up the grill for a two-level fire capable of cooking first on high heat (1 to 2 seconds with the hand test—see page 147) and then on medium (4 to 5 seconds with the hand test). If grilling over gas or charcoal, add a half-dozen mesquite chunks to the fire shortly before placing the steaks on the grill.

3. Grill the steaks over high heat for 2½ minutes per side. Move the steaks to medium heat, turning them again, and continue grilling for 2½ to 3 minutes per side for medium-rare. Serve immediately.

A WAGYU PRIMER

If you're a carnivore, you've likely heard of Wagyu beef, praised in almost reverent terms and priced like the jewelry at Neiman Marcus. What makes it so special? Marbling. So much marbling—and very fine, vein-like marbling too—giving the meat a pink color rather than the deeper red of domestic cattle breeds. Since fat is flavor, this Wagyu veining gives the meat an incomparable taste and great tenderness too. The fat itself is special as well, melting at a lower temperature so that it quite literally dissolves on the tongue for ultimate silky richness. The term Wagyu translates to "Japanese beef," but includes four different cattle breeds. Most Wagyu cattle are the Kurage breed, which is known for having the best intramuscular marbling of all the breeds. "Kobe beef" is a type of Wagyu from a specific prefecture in Japan. All Kobe is Wagyu, but not all Wagyu is Kobe. American Wagyu is a Wagyu cross-breed, usually with Angus, that must have at least 50% Wagyu genetics. Wagyu beef has its own numerical grading system. The highest—A5—is at least three grades higher than Prime beef, the highest grade ranked by the United States Department of Agriculture. One thing to remember with Wagyu is that the portion size is significantly different. It is so rich, only a couple of ounces will satisfy most anyone.

TEXAS STEAK MADE FAMOUS IN JAPAN

Most folks have to travel some distance to get to the Steakhouse. Would you believe that we have people fly in from Japan just to eat lunch or dinner? A few years ago, we had a crew from NHK, the PBS of Japan, come for a week and film all aspects of the Steakhouse and ranch. They put together a documentary about beef that featured three places in the world. The crew traveled to France to film a butcher, to Italy to feature the beloved bistecca alla Fiorentina, and to the Perini Ranch Steakhouse. We know that when we welcome our many Japanese guests, they will invariably order the bone-in ribeye because that's what the host of the program ate.

WET AND DRY AGING

Beef eats best after it has been aged, which can be done wet or dry. The process tenderizes the meat by allowing natural enzymes to break down the bonds that keep the muscle fibers tightly knit together, tenderizing the meat. Wet aging is the simpler of the two, meaning the meat is simply vacuum sealed and stored under refrigeration. Two weeks of wet aging is about the sweet spot says Jess Pryles, author of the *Hardcore Carnivore: Cook Meat Like You Mean It* cookbook and creator of the meat-centric website JessPryles.com. Dry aging lets the beef simply sit naked in a cool environment, which not only tenderizes the meat but allows it to develop deeper, funkier, almost blue cheese–like flavors. It's much more expensive because it seriously shrinks the weight, so that the price per pound goes up substantially. It also requires some additional trimming because the dry outer surface has to be cut off. Jess led a workshop at a recent Buffalo Gap Wine & Food Summit. She presented tastings of dry- and wet-aged beef, along with grass-finished versus grain-finished, and Wagyu alongside Angus and American Wagyu.

Beef Filets with Blue Cheese Butter

SERVES 6

BLUE CHEESE BUTTER

1 cup Danish blue cheese crumbles, at room temperature

½ cup (1 stick) salted butter, at room temperature

3 ounces cream cheese, at room temperature

2 teaspoons brine from a jar of pickled jalapeños

1 tablespoon minced fresh chives

1½ teaspoons fresh lemon juice

STEAK RUB

3 tablespoons kosher salt

1¾ teaspoons coarsely ground black pepper

½ teaspoon granulated garlic

½ teaspoon ground dried oregano

¼ teaspoon granulated onion

¼ teaspoon beef bouillon powder

Pinch of ground white pepper

Six 8-ounce center-cut tenderloin filets, each 1½ inches thick

Lots of folks love a filet because it's lean and cuts like butter. But without as much marbled fat as a ribeye, filet doesn't have quite as much flavor on its own, which is why it is often served with a béarnaise sauce. We agree emphatically that a filet needs extra fat for flavor, but we prefer to top each one with a generous slice of blue cheese butter. At the Steakhouse, we cut 8-ounce sections from the middle of the tenderloin for each diner.

1. **To Make the Blue Cheese Butter:** Combine the blue cheese, butter, cream cheese, brine, chives, and lemon juice in a food processor. Blend until combined. Transfer the butter mixture to a piece of waxed paper and roll the butter up in the paper into a 1-inch log. Refrigerate or freeze until needed.

2. **To Make the Rub:** Combine all the rub ingredients in a small bowl. Massage each filet generously with the rub. Let the steaks sit at room temperature for 30 minutes.

3. Fire up the grill for a two-level fire capable of cooking first on high heat (1 to 2 seconds with the hand test—see page 147) and then on medium (4 to 5 seconds with the hand test). For the best flavor, if cooking over gas or charcoal, add a half-dozen mesquite chunks to the fire shortly before placing the steaks on the grill.

4. Grill the filets uncovered over high heat for 1½ minutes per side. Move the filets to medium heat, turning them again, and continue grilling for 3½ to 4 minutes more per side for medium-rare doneness. Turn three times for grill marks. Serve immediately with a slice of blue cheese butter on top of each filet.

FIRING UP THE GRILL

Ever watched a group of guys standing around a hot fire while drinking beer, but ignoring the steaks on the grill? We'd hate to have them grilling our steaks. Grilling steaks to the right doneness requires your full attention and some basic skills. Like anything else, the more you do it, the easier it becomes and the better your steaks will be.

Knowing how to build a proper fire and how to control the heat are the first steps. Are you grilling or smoking? The main temperature variable is the quantity of fuel you use, which should always be relative to the size of the grill and the amount and type of food you're cooking.

Whether we are grilling, smoking, or cooking serious low-and-slow barbecue, we cook with mesquite wood because it's always been plentiful around these parts. These days, chefs grill with mesquite all over the country, but when Tom started this, it was considered "way out there." For all outdoor cooking, you want to burn a hardwood, like mesquite or oak, not resinous pine or cedar.

For grilling steaks or chops, we burn down fireplace-size mesquite logs to a certain level, but want active flames and high heat right under the meat. For smoked prime rib roast, we cook directly, but at a lower heat level—about 325°F—and over coals. For real barbecue, such as tough-as-a-blacksmith's-anvil pork ribs or beef brisket, the meat needs longer and lower cooking—250°F to 275°F—to develop succulence and tenderness under a coating of dried spices.

When we cater an event, we burn down logs in barrels we bring to the event (photo at left); the process always attracts the curious. We keep it behind the scenes at the Steakhouse so that no one singes their eyebrows or barbecues their boots.

We recommend using a charcoal chimney to start a fire. In a standard 22½-inch kettle-style grill, light 1½ charcoal-chimney loads of briquettes, lump charcoal, or hardwood chunks for four to six serious steaks. Briquettes reach a prime cooking temperature when they start to turn ashen, usually about 30 minutes after you light them. Lump charcoal and hardwood chunks usually ignite faster, get hotter, and burn more quickly. With any of the fuels, you can bump up the heat by bunching the coals together or opening the vents fully, or, if your grill provides the means, moving the food closer to the fire. To reduce the temperature, spread the coals apart, close or partially close the vents, or increase the distance between the food and the fire.

THE TWO-LEVEL FIRE

Thick steaks grill best on a two-level fire, where you can start the steaks over high heat and then finish them on medium. On gas grills with three or more burners, you can usually keep a hot fire and a medium fire going simultaneously from the beginning. On smaller grills, start hot and then turn down the heat at the appropriate point. On charcoal and wood-burning grills, establish two different cooking areas, one with coals in a single layer for moderate heat and another with coals piled two to three layers deep for a hot fire. An infrared burner, common on many high-end grills today, pumps out blazingly high heat for the first stage of cooking. Then grilling can be finished over medium heat on one of the grill's conventional burners.

THE HAND TEST

Our grilling recipes all recommend the "hand test" for gauging the heat of the fire, whether it be from gas, wood, or charcoal. While it might sound a little primitive for our technological age, it really does provide a more accurate measurement of heat than any modern gadget made for the grill. The thermometers built into today's grill hoods register only the oven heat when the cover is closed, not the true grilling temperature. In open grilling, the gauges don't measure a darned thing. The temperature knobs on your gas grills marked hot, medium, and low may provide more help over time, but not until you've determined how the settings compare with your hand measurements.

To test the temperature by hand, place your hand a couple of inches above the cooking grate and count the number of seconds before the heat of the fire forces you to pull your hand away. One to two seconds signifies high heat, perfect to start those steaks. Four to five seconds is medium, the level you want to finish the steaks.

Oven-Roasted Beef Tenderloin

SERVES 6

STEAK RUB

3 tablespoons kosher salt

1¾ teaspoons coarsely ground black pepper

½ teaspoon granulated garlic

½ teaspoon ground dried oregano

¼ teaspoon granulated onion

¼ teaspoon beef bouillon powder

Pinch of ground white pepper

One 2½-pound beef tenderloin, silverskin and surface fat removed

Extra virgin olive oil

When you want luscious beef for a dinner party but have limited time, or don't want to bother firing up the grill, here's the tenderloin for you. Our signature dry spice rub for steaks helps form a crust on the tenderloin and boosts the buttery meat's flavor without masking it.

Should you be lucky enough to have any leftovers, check out the ideas on page 150. When you want a simple appetizer to pass or for people to assemble themselves, each is a top choice, whether using this roasted tenderloin or a Mesquite Smoked Peppered Beef Tenderloin shipped from periniranch.com.

1. Heat the oven to 475°F. Combine all the rub ingredients in a small bowl. Brush the tenderloin lightly with a couple of teaspoons olive oil. Completely coat the tenderloin with all of the rub, pushing it into every little nook.

2. Rub a roasting rack with a teaspoon of oil so the meat and rub won't stick to it. Arrange the tenderloin on the rack and place in the roasting pan. Insert a meat thermometer into the thickest part of the tenderloin.

3. Plan on a total roasting time of 30 to 35 minutes. Place the tenderloin in the oven and cook for 10 minutes. Reduce the heat to 425°F and continue roasting for 20 to 25 minutes, until the thermometer reads 130°F (medium-rare). Transfer the meat to a cutting board and let it sit for 10 minutes before slicing.

Tenderloin Sliders (right): On each slider bun, arrange a slice or two of tenderloin, drizzle with horseradish sauce (1 cup sour cream mixed with 2 tablespoons prepared horseradish), and sprinkle with chopped parsley.

Beef Tenderloin and Guacamole Crostini: Start with small slices of toasted or grilled sourdough bread. Top each with a sliver of tenderloin, followed by a spoonful of Guacamole (page 61) and a sprinkle of crumbled queso fresco and chopped green onion.

Tenderloin-Arugula Wraps: For each, wrap a slice of tenderloin around a few arugula leaves, leaving a tuft of the leaves sticking out of one end. Use a toothpick to hold it together. Serve with Blue Cheese Dressing (page 102) for dipping.

Tenderloin-Remoulade Crostini: Spread some Remoulade (page 193) on crostini. Add a slice of tenderloin to each one, followed by a dot of remoulade. Garnish with some capers or lemon zest.

Tenderloin Bao Buns: Steam some frozen bao buns, then fill each with a couple of thin slices of tenderloin, a brush of hoisin sauce, and maybe a squirt of sriracha or other Asian chile paste. Tuck in a few fresh cilantro leaves too, if you like.

Tenderloin Bites: Using decorative toothpicks, skewer a slice of tenderloin (folded in thirds or quarters), a cherry tomato, and a pepperoncini pepper or a quarter of a seeded jalapeño.

Tenderloin-Potato Skewers: Make tiny skewers with a slice of tenderloin (folded in thirds or quarters) and steamed small new potatoes. Drizzle with a bit of pesto or serve with a bowl of Buttermilk Ranch Dressing (page 100).

HEAD OF THE CLASS

Back in 1989, Tom's friend Watt Matthews wanted to hold a special party for his Princeton class reunion. He asked us to fix a pit-roasted steer's head, an old South Texas barbecue specialty called barbacoa. Well sure, we said, we can do that! The only problem was that we had never seen one, much less cooked one. Since the request was made well before you could easily find information on the internet, the only reference we could come up with was from the epic Texas movie *Giant*. In the 1956 film, Leslie Lynnton Benedict, Elizabeth Taylor's character, fainted at the sight of the cooked steer's head, which perhaps should have been a harbinger to us of things to come.

We dug a hefty hole in the ground for the pit/oven, built a wood fire, and cooked the canvas-wrapped steer head on the hot coals for 18 hours. When it was time to pull it out, all these Princeton-educated CEOs were watching with great excitement and curiosity. We acted like we haul cow heads out of pits every day. With great fanfare, we dug up the thing, then unwrapped it and plopped it on a table. As Tom remembered from the movie, we broke it open with a hatchet and served it straight out of the skull. People lined up and we offered them pit-cooked meat from the head and scoops of the brains. We smiled and carried on as if this was utterly normal for us. One of the wives reacted—almost—in Liz Taylor style. She didn't end up fainting, but she just couldn't deal with it. After apologizing, she headed over to the calf fries and put a great big helping on her plate. No one had the heart to tell her what she was enjoying.

Ranch Roasted Prime Rib

SERVES 8 OR MORE

PRIME RIB RUB

½ cup coarsely ground black pepper

¼ cup kosher salt

1 tablespoon plus 1 teaspoon garlic powder

1 tablespoon plus 1 teaspoon crumbled dried oregano

One 4-rib rib roast (prime rib), about 8 pounds, bones removed

Logs to fuel a wood-burning smoker, mesquite if available

For a special occasion, few cuts of beef are more visually striking than a prime rib roast. You ought to see it when we lay out forty of them side-by-side for big parties! At the Perini Ranch, we actually have enough barbecue pits to smoke-roast prime rib for 1,200 lucky folks. When our crew slices the beef, it further wows diners because each slice covers most of a plate. It's worth noting that "prime rib" is the full rack from which ribeye steaks are cut. When cut into individual steaks, you get more crustiness in proportion to the meat because a steak is grilled on both sides, but a large prime rib is going to brown just on the outer edges. Both can be delicious. It's a personal preference. We like more pepper in our prime rib rub because, with its higher fat content and larger surface area, the prime rib can handle a more piquant rub.

1. Combine all the rub ingredients in a small bowl and mix well. Place the roast on a baking sheet. Massage the dry rub all over the roast, really packing it on. Let sit at room temperature while getting the smoker ready.

2. Fire up the smoker, bringing the temperature to 300°F to 325°F. Logs should be burned down to large coals before adding them to the fire. You will want to do this in some kind of fireproof barrel or tub. Add more coals as needed throughout the hours of smoking to maintain the proper temperature.

3. Before cooking, take the internal temperature of the meat, deep in the roast's center, with an instant-read thermometer. The temperature should be nearing 40°F, considered the high end of the safe range for beef to sit out unrefrigerated. If the temperature of the roast is more than a couple of degrees below 40°F, plan to extend the cooking time by a few minutes.

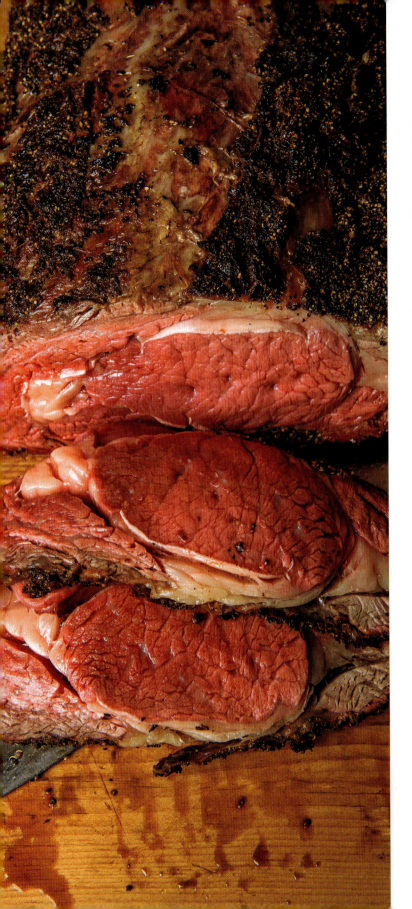

4. Transfer the prime rib to the smoker, fattier side up. Plan on a total cooking time of 2 to 2½ hours. After 1½ hours, check the internal temperature, deep in the roast's center again, to gauge the rest of the cooking time. You don't want to overcook a piece of meat this special. We prefer to take the roast off when it is in the rare to medium-rare range, 120°F to 130°F. We don't advise cooking it beyond 140°F, the high side of medium. (Although you might want to cook the roast just to 140°F, so that you have prime rib of varying doneness.)

5. Tent the roast loosely with aluminum foil and let sit for 30 minutes. Allowing the roast to rest is essential, so all the meat's juices settle and aren't lost when the roast is sliced. Carve into thick slices and serve.

COLD PRIME RIB ON TOASTED SOURDOUGH WITH HORSERADISH SAUCE: For each sandwich, toast two thin slices of sourdough bread. Lay out one piece of toast and slather one side with horseradish sauce (1 cup sour cream mixed with 2 tablespoons prepared horseradish). Arrange a slice of cold prime rib over the sauce. Add a couple of red-ripe tomato slices and crisp romaine leaves or other lettuce. Top with the remaining slice of toast, smeared with a little more horseradish sauce if you're as crazy for horseradish as we are. Such good eating.

OPEN-FACED HOT PRIME RIB SANDWICHES WITH MELTED CHEDDAR, GRILLED MUSHROOMS, AND ONIONS: Toss thick slices of button mushrooms with thin slices of onion and enough melted butter or vegetable oil to coat them. Grill the vegetables over medium heat or sauté in a medium skillet until tender. Arrange one slice of white bread per person on a baking sheet. Top each one with a slice of prime rib. Spoon on the mushrooms and onion slices. Top with 2 slices medium or sharp Cheddar cheese. Bake at 450°F for 3 to 5 minutes, until the cheese is melting and gooey.

OUR MOST MEMORABLE CATERING JOB

When Governor George W. Bush was inaugurated as President Bush "43" in 2001, we dreamed that someday we might have the opportunity to cater an event at the White House. We got The Call later that spring, requesting a Texas-size and Texas-themed bash for the annual Congressional Picnic in September. We were asked to haul chuck wagons, handcrafted barbecue pits, a trailer full of mesquite, a crew of cowboys, and anything else needed to create an authentic Lone Star feast on the South Lawn of the White House. Austin-based Ray Benson and his band Asleep at the Wheel would be entertaining the 1,400 expected guests, which included all members of the House and Senate and their families. In June, we made a trip to D.C. to work out the details and logistics with the White House chefs and staff. We told them we planned to serve bread pudding, green chile hominy, Southern green beans cooked with bacon drippings, and Mesquite Smoked Peppered Beef Tenderloin. The executive chef looked incredulous, and finally he blurted out that we would have to serve chicken. "You're in Washington!" That sucked the air right out of the room. Tom countered with, "When you're serving a Texas chuck wagon meal, you serve beef. If you want another main course, I'll do catfish." It took a consultation with the First Lady, but the menu was approved with all our suggested dishes, plus fried catfish.

We arrived in Washington for the long-planned event on Sunday, September 9. Early the next day we began working with the staff on the food preparation and setting up all the equipment, which included 160 picnic tables. We were up early on the morning of September 11, ready for the big day. While Lisa was still getting dressed, Tom sat down to watch some TV to calm his nerves. What he saw in no way calmed his nerves; in fact, it was downright horrifying. It was the planes flying into the World Trade Center's Twin Towers in New York. Looking out the hotel window at the sparkling blue-sky fall day made it all the more incomprehensible. We opened the window and immediately smelled smoke. It was coming from the Pentagon, where another plane had crashed.

Later in the day, a call came from the White House about whether we could give the food for the cancelled party to the firefighters and other first responders. Of course. Then we offered to come over and start the BBQ pits, but it was

pointed out that smoke coming from the White House lawn might cause further panic, and that we certainly couldn't do anything that would look festive, so the food was prepared indoors by the White House kitchen staff.

The following day, we were back outside the White House, packing up everything that had been set up on Monday. Tom heard a whistle and his name called out and looked up to see President Bush striding toward him. Now, there's a protocol that you never approach the president; it makes those Secret Service folks real nervous. But we walked up to the commander-in-chief, who, in the midst of the country's biggest crisis, commented that he was sorry we had not been able to cater the party. He also said we'd plan it again because he wasn't going to let terrorists change the way we live our lives. As the president headed back inside, one of our cowboys hollered out, "We'll be praying for you, Mr. President." He stopped and turned around and said, "Thank you. I need that." And then the most powerful man in the world slipped back into his office to deal with our new reality. True to his promise, we were back at the White House the following year when the tradition of the Congressional Picnic resumed.

West Texas Mesquite Smoked Brisket

SERVES 12 TO 15

One 8- to 12-pound packer-trimmed beef brisket

BRISKET RUB

¼ cup plus 2 tablespoons coarse ground black pepper

¼ cup chili powder

¼ cup kosher salt

2 tablespoons garlic powder

2 tablespoons onion powder

BRISKET MOP

1½ cups vegetable oil or rendered beef tallow

1½ cups white vinegar

½ medium red onion, cut into 4 pieces

2 medium lemons, halved

Logs to fuel a wood-burning smoker, mesquite if available

We cook our wildly popular smoked briskets for special events and catered parties. You can mail order it any time of the year from periniranch.com, but here's our technique if you'd like to make it for yourself. It takes about 12 hours—about as long as it takes to drink two 6-packs of beer, according to our crew—to smoke a full "packer-trimmed" brisket, the style that includes both the point and flat cuts.

I'd like to give credit here to my friend Cliff Teinert, from Albany, Texas. In the 1970s, we cooked together a lot and it's from Cliff that I learned about correctly making coals and cooking on pits, especially when it comes to brisket. We cook them West Texas style, which involves burning mesquite logs down to coals, and then cooking the meat low and slow at a temperature of 250°F to 275°F. While the briskets are cooking, we "mop" them with a mixture of oil or rendered beef fat, vinegar, and some seasonings, which keeps the meat moist and adds a layer of flavor. We strive for a good hit of smokiness from the fire, but not so much smoke that it masks the brisket's classic beefiness. We leave off any accompanying sauce for the same reason. Depending on your smoker and the size of your crowd, you might want to do a second brisket at the same time. If you don't have a smoker or barbecue pit of some kind, or a heavy-duty grill, try the oven variation.

Barbecued brisket was one of those dishes Tom figured out early. Initially he would prepare it the old-time way, digging a hole in the ground and filling it with those mesquite coals mentioned above. "We'd stretch what's called bull wire across the pit, so that the brisket would be sitting about three feet above those coals, then we'd turn them when the time seemed just right. That was back when we'd just do a couple of briskets at a time, but never know if we'd have enough diners coming in to finish them off." Now it's not uncommon for us to cook 50 briskets at a time.

1. Trim the brisket of any large pieces of fat or membrane. Turn so the fat-covered side is up. Trim the surface fat to an even ¼ to ½ inch. Cut out any visible pieces of hard fat where the point and flat portions of the brisket meet. Place the brisket on a baking sheet.

2. To Make the Rub: Combine all the rub ingredients in a small bowl.

3. Apply the rub evenly to the brisket, massaging it into every crevice. Let the brisket sit on a baking sheet at room temperature for up to an hour while preparing the smoker.

4. Fire up the smoker, bringing the temperature to 250°F to 275°F. Logs should be burned down to large coals before adding them to the fire. You will want to do this in some kind of fireproof barrel or tub. Add more coals as needed throughout the hours of smoking to maintain the proper temperature.

5. To Make the Mop: Combine 1½ cups hot water, oil, vinegar, onion, and lemon halves in a medium saucepan over low heat and heat until warmed.

6. Put the brisket, fat-side up, directly on the smoker grate. Cook the brisket until well done and very tender, 1 to 1¼ hours per pound. An 8-pound brisket will take 9 to 10 hours, while a 12-pound one will require at least 12 hours. Once an hour, baste the brisket with the mop and turn it. Keep the mop warm. If it begins to run low, add more hot water or make another batch. When the brisket is cooked, it should have a dark crust, almost like black bark, and its internal temperature should read 190°F to 200°F on an instant-read thermometer.

7. Once the brisket is cooked, transfer it from the smoker to a platter. If you are planning to serve the meat within 30 to 45 minutes, let it sit at room temperature. If it will be longer, wrap the meat in a couple of layers of uncoated butcher or parchment paper. (Don't use aluminum foil; it will steam the meat and soften the desirable crust.)

8. Slice the meat thinly against the grain, down through both the fattier point and leaner flat cut portions of meat. Watch as you work, though, because the grain changes directions. Serve immediately.

OVEN-ROASTED BRISKET: While this version lacks the serious crustiness achieved in a smoker over some dozen hours, the coarsely ground pepper adds a lot of character. If you use a smoked pepper, such as Whiskey Barrel Smoked Black Pepper from savoryspice.com, you'll add another delicious layer of flavor. Start with a 4-pound brisket flat cut. Put the brisket in a roasting pan. Make just half of the rub and massage it into the brisket. Bake uncovered for 1 hour at 350°F. Pour 1½ cups beef stock around the brisket and add water as needed to equal about ½ inch of liquid in the pan. Cover the pan tightly. Reduce the temperature to 325°F and continue baking for about 3 more hours, until fork-tender.

THE MYSTIQUE OF MESQUITE

At the Steakhouse, we use mesquite because it's a native Texas tree that grows all around us. Originally, we gathered the wood at the ranch and even chopped it ourselves. Now we go through so much of it that we have it delivered twenty cords at a time. It has to be very dry. Some of our mesquite has been aged for ten years or more, so that the tar and pitch are long gone. It's an excellent high-heat wood for grilling and gives off a fragrant woodsy aroma you immediately associate with the West. To smoke or barbecue with it, you want to burn it down to coals before you start, otherwise the smoke can get acrid over the long time needed to cook, say, a brisket. Foodways Texas and Texas A&M University host an annual Camp Brisket for passionate barbecue fans. Participants learn every detail about cooking the challenging beef cut, including the best woods to use. Each year, there's a side-by-side tasting of brisket cooked over various woods. Mesquite is always at or near the top in the blind taste testing.

Chicken-Fried Steak with Cream Gravy

SERVES 4

1¾ to 2 pounds beef tenderloin, cut into 4 equal portions, trimmed of all sinew and fat

¾ cup whole milk

1 large egg, beaten

2 teaspoons kosher salt

½ teaspoon freshly ground black pepper

2 cups all-purpose flour

Vegetable oil or shortening, for frying

CREAM GRAVY

3 tablespoons all-purpose flour

2 cups cold whole milk

Kosher salt and freshly ground black pepper

We can't overstate the importance of chicken-fried steak to Texas culture. In 2011, October 26 was proclaimed Texas Chicken Fried Steak Day by the state legislature. It's a holiday on our calendar and we serve tons of CFS to honor the day. The dish has been handed down from the 19th-century heyday of cattle drives and cowboys. Cattle drives aren't such a big deal today, but we get plenty of Texas folks who think nothing of driving several hours for a great meal. In fact, people come from all across Texas and beyond to enjoy this golden-fried, crusty slab of steak, which is served only at our Sunday buffet, and of course, on October 26. Most restaurants and recipes use round steak (a rear-end cut with little marbling), but at the Steakhouse, we prefer tenderloins for our "chicken-fried."

Both of us, at separate times, have been president of the Texas Restaurant Association, the only husband-and-wife team to have held that honor. One of the handy statistics that the association came up with is that some 90 percent of Texas restaurants serve chicken-fried steak. We're not sure that even 90 percent would say they serve coffee. You'll want some Mashed Potatoes (page 222) along with this to sop up the cream gravy, which also goes well generously spooned over Buttermilk Biscuits (page 240) and The Judge's Fried Chicken (page 180).

1. Using a meat mallet, pound the steak pieces ¼-inch thick. Whisk together the milk, egg, salt, and pepper in a shallow bowl. Spread the flour in another shallow bowl. One at a time, dredge the steak pieces in the egg-milk mixture, then in the flour. Repeat dredging in the liquid and then the flour. The surface of the meat should be fairly dry.

2. Clip a deep-fry thermometer to the inside of a deep 12- or 14-inch cast-iron skillet or Dutch oven. Pour in oil to a depth of 1 inch and bring the temperature of the oil to 325°F over medium-high heat. Line a baking sheet with paper towels. Put a wire baking rack on top of the paper towels.

3. When the oil is hot, add the steaks, in batches if necessary. In 4 to 5 minutes, when the meat juices start to pool on top of each piece and the bottoms are golden brown, turn the steaks and cook until golden brown, 4 to 5 minutes more. Drain the steaks on the rack and transfer to a warm platter. Keep them warm while you prepare the gravy.

4. **To Make the Gravy:** Pour off the fat from the pan through a strainer, leaving ¼ cup fat and pan drippings in the bottom of the skillet, discarding the rest. Return any browned cracklings in the strainer to the skillet. Warm the pan drippings over medium heat. Add the flour, whisking to avoid lumps. Add the milk, whisking frequently, bring to a simmer, and cook until the gravy is thickened, about 3 minutes.

Stir the gravy up from the bottom frequently, scraping up the browned bits. Add salt and a good amount of pepper so the cream gravy has more than a suspicion of pepper. Taste for seasoning. Pour the gravy over the steaks or on the side and serve immediately.

Texas Chili

SERVES 8 OR MORE

4 pounds chili-grind beef with 20% fat content

1 large onion, diced

1 tablespoon minced garlic

3 tablespoons chili powder

1 tablespoon ground cumin

1 teaspoon crumbled dried oregano

1 cup Pace Picante Sauce, preferably medium heat

1 cup diced tomatoes (about 1 large), or 1 cup canned diced tomatoes with juice

Kosher salt and freshly ground black pepper

1 jalapeño, minced

Back in 1977, our Texas legislature saw fit to make chili the state dish. There was, however, precious little agreement on the ingredients and best recipe. The only thing all Texans can assent to is that Texas chili does not include beans. Be sure, though, to include some of our state pepper, the jalapeño; and, if you wish, cook it in our official state cooking implement, the cast-iron Dutch oven.

"Chili-grind" beef is a good bit coarser than meat ground for burgers. It's ground daily that way in many Texas markets, and can usually be requested anywhere that has a meat department. It's very important to get the right texture for the chili. Accompany each serving with a wedge of Skillet Cornbread (page 249) or Cheddar-Jalapeño Cornbread (page 250).

1. Combine the beef, onion, and garlic in a large Dutch oven and cook over medium-high heat, stirring frequently, until evenly browned. Stir in the chili powder, cumin, oregano, picante sauce, tomatoes and juice, and 2 cups hot water. Bring to a boil over medium-high heat. Reduce the heat to a simmer, cover, and cook for 1 hour, stirring frequently, until the chili thickens.

2. Add at least 1 teaspoon salt, a few grinds of pepper, and the jalapeño and cook for 15 minutes. Taste again and if needed, add a bit more salt or pepper, and cook for another few minutes.

3. Serve piping hot in bowls. The chili can be cooled, covered, and refrigerated overnight, and reheated or frozen.

BISON CHILI: Use 3 pounds coarsely ground bison and 1 pound ground beef. The beef is fattier than the bison and gives bison chili a richer mouthfeel.

Carne Guisada

2½ pounds beef tenderloin, cut in inch-size cubes

2 tablespoons all-purpose flour

1 tablespoon table salt, or more to taste

3 tablespoons beef tallow or extra virgin olive oil

1 cup chopped onion

1 tablespoon minced garlic

One 15-ounce can diced tomatoes, fire-roasted if available

2 cups beef stock

1 tablespoon chili powder

2 teaspoons ground cumin

2 teaspoons paprika

Flour tortillas, warmed, for serving

Guisadas or *guisados* are stew-like dishes from Mexico and other Latin countries. Ours has a distinct Tex-Mex chili powder- and cumin-based flair. It also has some Perini flair because—while most guisadas are made with beef chuck or other meat requiring long cooking to become tender—we make this with trimming from our tenderloins. It makes the cooking much quicker as well as luscious. The flavor is somewhat classic chili-like, but the meat is in larger cubes, is flavored more heavily with tomatoes, and the mixture remains soupier than a Texas chili.

1. Heat the oven to 300°F. Dust the meat cubes with the flour and salt. Warm the beef tallow or oil in a heavy ovenproof saucepan or Dutch oven over medium-high heat. Brown the beef in batches quickly on the cooktop. Scoop out each batch as it is browned and transfer to a plate.

2. Add the onion and garlic and continue cooking over medium heat until the onion is softened and translucent, scraping up any browned bits from the bottom. Stir the beef and any juices back into the pan and add the remaining ingredients.

3. Cover and bake for 50 to 60 minutes, until the flavors in the sauce have melded and the beef is very tender. Taste and add more salt, if you wish. If sauce seems thin, transfer pan to the cooktop and simmer over medium-low a few minutes until thickened.

4. Serve in bowls with flour tortillas on the side.

LISA'S PRO TIP: A carne guisada burrito, with salsa, cures all problems on a cold morning!

Beef Fajitas

SERVES 6

Two 1- to 1¼-pound skirt steaks, trimmed of membranes and excess fat

1 tablespoon kosher salt

1 tablespoon coarsely ground black pepper

Guacamole (page 61), for serving

Pico de Gallo (page 60) or other salsa, for serving

Shredded Cheddar or Monterey Jack cheese, for serving

12 flour tortillas, warmed, for serving

It's hard to imagine that grilled skirt steak wrapped in tortillas was little known beyond the Rio Grande Valley's vaqueros, or cowboys, until the 1970s. That's when Texas restaurants and food booths at fairs and festivals caught on and fajitas became popular; they've been on our catering menu since the Steakhouse opened in 1983.

Folks sometimes prepare fajitas with flank steak or even sirloin, but we prefer the classic long, flat, and beefy skirt steak. While all steaks should be sliced against, not with, the grain, it's essential to do so with skirt steak, or the slices will be tough and stringy rather than tender. Ask your butcher for "inside" skirt; it's a little more tender and will cost a bit more, but it's worth it.

1. Cut each steak in half to make shorter, more manageable pieces of the meat. Combine the salt and pepper and rub them into the meat. Let the steaks sit uncovered at room temperature while preparing the grill.

2. Fire up the grill for a two-level fire capable of cooking on high (1 to 2 seconds with the hand test—see page 147) and medium heat (4 to 5 seconds with the hand test) at the same time. If grilling over gas or charcoal, add a half-dozen mesquite chunks to the fire shortly before placing the steaks on the grill.

3. Grill the steaks over high heat for 3 to 4 minutes per side if less than ½ inch thick, or 4 to 5 minutes per side if more than ½ inch thick, until medium-rare. Turn the steaks more often if juice pools on the surface. Tent with aluminum foil and let rest for 5 minutes.

4. Holding a knife at a slight diagonal, slice the steaks across the grain into thin finger-length strips.

5. To serve, pile the steak strips on a platter, accompanied by bowls of guacamole, salsa, and shredded cheese, and a napkin-lined basket of warm tortillas.

SERVES 4

CHIPOTLE SAUCE

2 chipotle chiles and 1 tablespoon adobo sauce from a can of chipotles in adobo

1 ripe red tomato, chopped

1 tablespoon minced onion

1 garlic clove, minced

½ cup water

Table salt and freshly ground black pepper

CRUNCHY SLAW

2 cups coleslaw mix (shredded cabbage with carrots)

¼ cup mayonnaise

1 tablespoon granulated sugar

2 teaspoons fresh lemon juice

2 teaspoons apple cider vinegar

¼ teaspoon table salt

¼ teaspoon freshly ground black pepper

CARAMELIZED ONIONS

2 teaspoons vegetable oil

1 medium onion, halved and sliced into thin half-moons

Table salt

¾ pound Perini Ranch Mesquite Smoked Peppered Beef Tenderloin, sliced thin, at room temperature

8 to 12 soft corn tortillas, warmed

Slices of avocado, chopped fresh onion, fresh cilantro leaves, optional

Carne Asada Tacos

Any dish where grilled beef is traditionally at its center is likely something we've tried with our Mesquite Smoked Peppered Beef Tenderloin. This combination has become especially popular, drizzled with a smoky chipotle chile sauce. It's now in regular rotation as part of The Gap Café's lunch menu. We put a crunchy slaw on the side, but since lots of folks put it on the tacos, we're including it here too.

1. To Make the Chipotle Sauce: Combine the ingredients in a small saucepan. Bring to a boil, then reduce the heat to a simmer and cook for 10 to 12 minutes, until the tomato and onion have softened. Spoon the mixture into a food processor and puree it. Set the sauce aside.

2. To Make the Slaw: In a medium bowl, stir together all of the ingredients. Refrigerate until needed.

3. To Make the Caramelized Onions: Warm the oil in a small skillet over medium heat, then add the onion. Cover to sweat the mixture for about 5 minutes, until the onion has softened. Uncover and sauté for about 5 minutes more, stirring occasionally, until the onion is quite soft and lightly colored.

4. For each taco, arrange on a corn tortilla a portion of the meat, caramelized onions, and sauce. If you wish, dress with avocado, raw onion, and cilantro. Add slaw, if you like, or put it on the side. Serve right away.

TOM'S TIP: Did you know we have actual scientific data to prove how tender beef and other meat is? Meat scientists use a shear force test to measure the resistance of meat, so we can rank the tenderness of different steaks. The tenderloin is well named, coming out at the top of the tenderness scale, one of the reasons it can be cooked fast and hot and served quite rare. As you might guess, brisket and chuck are among the toughest, needing long, low cooking to coax them into tasty submission.

The *TODAY* Show Award-Winning Ranch Burgers

SERVES 6

RUB

3 tablespoons kosher salt

1¾ teaspoons coarsely ground black pepper

½ teaspoon granulated garlic

½ teaspoon ground dried oregano

¼ teaspoon granulated onion

¼ teaspoon beef bouillon powder

Pinch of ground white pepper

BURGERS

3 pounds freshly ground chuck with 20% fat content

Vegetable oil (if cooking in a skillet)

6 sturdy burger buns, halved

6 slices medium Cheddar or provolone cheese, at room temperature

4 ounces thinly sliced button mushrooms, grilled or sautéed

¾ to 1 cup chopped fresh-roasted or jarred New Mexico green chiles

Mustard or mayonnaise, tomato slices, iceberg lettuce leaves, grilled thin onion slices, pickle slices

A dozen or so years ago, we decided our burger needed an upgrade. We dissected every element of it, from bun to burger to condiments. We experimented cooking burgers on a griddle vs. a grill. We cooked them at different temperatures. We finally built our perfect burger, and it wasn't long after that *Food Network Magazine* proclaimed it to be the best burger in all of Texas. *Texas Monthly* chimed in, elevating the burger to its best burger list as well. The staff of NBC's *TODAY* show was scouring America's best burger lists to run a competition at Rockefeller Plaza, where the show tapes in New York City. They invited us to compete against other cooks. Most of the other burgers and cooking techniques were way over the top. One was even called Heart Attack on a Plate. We called them "all hat, no cattle." Tom set up a small three-legged grill and cooked what we do best: A Ranch Burger with fresh-roasted green chiles, grilled mushrooms, onions, and some sliced cheese. The judges chose Tom's no-frills burger as the winner!

A burger is only as good as its parts. Everything counts, from the ground chuck to the cheese to the bun. The bun should have enough firmness to stand up to the meat patty but should also feel soft when lightly pressed. Pass on wimpy buns that fall apart under the heft and the juiciness of the burger. Our slightly sweet sourdough buns come from Sheila Partin's Sweet Mesquite Bakery in Houston. You can order these white sandwich buns online at sbakery.com.

Directions follow for cooking these on a grill or in a cast-iron skillet. No matter which cooking method you choose, avoid mashing the burgers down with a spatula; delicious juices will be lost.

1. To Make the Rub: Combine all the ingredients in a large bowl. Add the ground chuck and, using clean hands, mix well.

2. To Make the Burgers: Divide and shape the beef into 6 equal balls. Pat each ball into ¾-inch-thick patties. Handle gently, so that the burgers hold together but are somewhat loose, not firmly packed.

3. To Grill the Burgers: Fire up the grill for a two-level fire capable of cooking first on high heat (1 to 2 seconds with the hand test—see page 147) and then on medium heat (4 to 5 seconds with the hand test). For best flavor if cooking over gas or charcoal, add a half-dozen mesquite chunks to the fire a few minutes before putting the burgers on the grill.

Grill the burgers over high heat for 1½ minutes per side. Move the burgers to medium heat and rotate a half-turn for grill marks. Cook for an additional 3½ to 4 minutes per side, until crusty on the outside and with a bare hint of pink at the center for medium, or more or less to desired doneness.

4. Place the bottom of a bun on a plate. Arrange a cheeseburger patty on top of the bun. Spoon on the mushrooms and green chiles. Place the bun top and all the other condiments on the side and serve.

5. To Cook the Burgers in a Skillet: Heat a large cast-iron skillet over high heat. Add just enough oil to coat the bottom of the skillet. Turn the heat down to medium and rotate skillet around to distribute the oil. Add three of the burgers, if they fit without crowding. Cook for 3 minutes and turn once. Place a slice of cheese on top of each burger and cook until medium-rare, about 3 minutes longer. Cook the second batch of burgers.

Smashburgers

SERVES 4

SMASHBURGER SAUCE

¾ cup mayonnaise

2 tablespoon Worcestershire sauce

1 tablespoon ketchup

½ teaspoon ground black pepper

1½ pounds freshly ground chuck with 20% fat content

1 teaspoon table salt

1 teaspoon freshly ground black pepper

1 tablespoon beef tallow or vegetable oil

8 slices American cheese, at room temperature

4 potato rolls, split, or other sturdy burger buns

Shredded iceberg lettuce, slices of mild onion such as Texas 1015, dill pickle slices, or—in season—slices of red-ripe tomatoes, optional

In our classic grilled burger, we always make the point of NOT pressing down on the beef patties, so that juices aren't lost and the texture remains tender. Smashburgers toss that wisdom out the window. Smashing creates more surface area to develop a deeply browned exterior, and by doubling up each bun with a pair of skinny burgers, it also doubles that crusty goodness. Cook these on a griddle or in a large cast-iron skillet, using a sturdy offset spatula to smash the burger patties as well as scrape them up with all their crispy bits. A good kitchen ventilation fan is a plus! These are cooked fairly well-done, unlike our grilled burgers, but the cheese and special sauce help keep everything moist and tasty.

1. Place the mayonnaise, Worcestershire, ketchup, and pepper in a bowl and stir to combine. Set the sauce aside. Mix together the ground chuck, salt, and pepper. Form the mixture into 8 balls.

2. Heat a griddle or large cast-iron skillet over high heat for 3 minutes. Just before you transfer the beef patties to the griddle, add a tablespoon of beef tallow or oil to the griddle. Cook as many burgers as you can at a time, eyeballing how many mashed patties will fill the space. Transfer the balls of meat to the griddle and, working quickly, smash them as fully as you can, to about ⅓-inch in thickness. The edges will get lacy and crisp. Cook for about 1 minute, until the bottom is richly browned, then scrape up and turn over. Smash down again, then immediately top each burger with a slice of cheese. Continue cooking about 30 seconds to 1 minute more. The burgers should be crusty and richly browned. Stack two cheese-covered burgers on top of each other. Repeat with remaining burgers.

3. Smear the buns with sauce. Place a pair of cheese-covered burgers on each bun bottom. Add other garnishes, if you wish. Crown with bun tops. Eat the burgers right away, squeezing buns gently to mingle the juices, cheesy gooeyness, and sauce.

NOT BEEF

Cattle ranchers are loyal to beef at the center of the plate. Remember the phrase from the Texas Beef Council, "Beef. It's what's for dinner." That said, even we occasionally put something else at the center of our plates, a delicious variation that perks up the tastebuds.

Mesquite Smoked Pork Ribs

RIB RUB

2 tablespoons coarsely ground black pepper

2 tablespoons sweet paprika

1 tablespoon kosher salt

1½ teaspoons dry mustard

1½ teaspoons garlic powder

¾ teaspoon cayenne

Two 2-pound slabs pork back ribs or St. Louis cut spareribs (trimmed of chine bones and brisket flap), preferably from a heritage pork breed, such as Duroc or Berkshire

Logs to fuel a wood-burning smoker, mesquite if available

Pork ribs have always been popular on the Texas barbecue scene. Our ribs are rubbed with spices and smoked, then served without sauce. Look for Duroc, Berkshire, or other well-marbled heritage pork ribs. Use either back or spareribs. With spareribs, ask your butcher to cut them St. Louis style, which removes a cartilage-loaded portion of the sternum and an odd tough bit of flap meat. The cut also squares up the rack, making it easier to cook, slice, and eat. We burn down mesquite logs, and then cook the ribs directly over smoking white-hot coals at 250°F for 3 to 3½ hours.

1. Combine all the rub ingredients in a small bowl. Massage both sides of the rib racks with the rub. Let the ribs sit at room temperature for 30 minutes.

2. Fire up a smoker, bringing its temperature to 225°F to 250°F. Logs should be burned down to large coals in some kind of fireproof barrel or tub before adding them to the fire. Add more coals as needed throughout the hours of smoking to maintain the proper temperature.

3. Transfer the ribs to the smoker, meaty sides up, and cook for 3 hours. Turn the rib racks over and cook for another 30 minutes. They are ready when you pick up a rack from the center with tongs and it relaxes and droops. The meat should pull easily from the bones but be short of falling off. Cut the ribs parallel to the bones into individual pieces. Serve immediately with plenty of napkins.

OVEN-BAKED SPARE RIBS: Heat the oven to 225°F. Rub the ribs with the dry rub as described above. As with the oven-baked brisket, using a smoked pepper will add a good hit of extra flavor. Place the ribs close together on a baking sheet lined with a silicone mat. Cover the baking sheet with foil and bake for 2½ hours. Uncover and bake for about 1 hour longer. They are ready when you pick up a rack from the center with tongs and it relaxes and droops. The meat should pull easily from the bones but be short of falling off.

Braised Bison Short Ribs

SERVES 4 TO 6

4 pounds meaty bone-in English-cut bison or beef short ribs

2 medium tomatoes, halved through their equators

2 jalapeños, halved lengthwise

1 large onion, quartered

8 ounces button mushrooms, halved if large

3 green onions, chopped

1 cup plus ½ cup dry red wine, such as Cabernet Sauvignon or Merlot

4 cups low-sodium beef stock

⅓ cup Worcestershire sauce

1 bay leaf

1 tablespoon onion powder

1½ teaspoons kosher salt, or more to taste

½ teaspoon granulated garlic

½ teaspoon ground white pepper

½ teaspoon crumbled dried oregano

¼ teaspoon whole black peppercorns

¼ cup cornstarch

Buffalo once did roam through Buffalo Gap, coming to drink at nearby Elm Creek. We created this hearty dish for the Comanche Moon Social, an annual local fundraiser for the Buffalo Gap Historic Village, where Tom served on the board. A Comanche moon refers to the bright full moon that warriors preferred for their fearsome raids. Bison ribs are leaner and more expensive than readily available beef ribs; either will work here, although beef ribs are more sizeable so you may need to add about 30 minutes to the baking time. We like short ribs with a side of Mashed Potatoes (page 222) and some crusty bread.

1. Heat the oven to 325°F. Place the short ribs, tomatoes, jalapeños, onion, mushrooms, and green onions in a Dutch oven or stockpot. Add 1 cup of the wine, the stock, Worcestershire, bay leaf, onion powder, salt, garlic, white pepper, oregano, and peppercorns. Bring to a simmer over high heat, cover, and transfer to the oven. Bake for 2 to 2½ hours, until the meat is pull-apart tender when pierced with a fork.

2. Using tongs, transfer the ribs to a platter and cover with aluminum foil. Strain the cooking liquid through a large fine-mesh strainer into a large saucepan. Using the back of a wooden spoon, press down on the vegetables to get every bit of flavor and juice from them. Discard the vegetables in the strainer.

3. Bring the cooking liquid to a boil over medium-high heat. Lower the heat and simmer to reduce the sauce by about one-third, 10 to 15 minutes. Whisk together the remaining ½ cup wine and the cornstarch in a bowl so there are no lumps. Stir the wine-cornstarch mixture into the sauce. Continue cooking until the sauce thickens, 2 to 3 minutes longer.

4. While the sauce is reducing, use two forks to pull the meat from the bones. Discard the bones and cartilage. Add the meat to the sauce, heat through, and serve.

Grilled Lamb Chops with Jalapeño Jelly

SERVES 6

LAMB CHOP RUB

1 tablespoon kosher salt

½ teaspoon coarsely ground black pepper

¼ teaspoon granulated garlic

¼ teaspoon ground dried oregano

6 single-cut frenched lamb chops

Jalapeño jelly, warmed

Frenched lamb chops are cleaned of fat on the rib bones, making them easy to pick up and eat with your fingers. We cover them with steak rub and, once nicely charred, serve with jalapeño jelly. We prefer to buy lamb that hasn't been shipped frozen from the other side of the world, since there's plenty of delicious meat available from American ranchers.

1. Combine all the rub ingredients in a small bowl. Massage each chop generously with the dry rub. Let the chops sit at room temperature for 30 minutes.

2. Fire up the grill for a two-level fire capable of cooking first on high heat (1 to 2 seconds with the hand test—see page 147) and then on medium (4 to 5 seconds with the hand test). For the best flavor if cooking over gas or charcoal, add a half-dozen mesquite chunks to the fire shortly before placing the chops on the grill.

3. Grill the chops over high heat for 1½ to 2 minutes per side. Move the chops to medium heat, turning them again, and continue grilling for 2 to 2½ minutes per side for medium-rare. Serve immediately, with a side of jelly.

The Judge's Fried Chicken

SERVES 4 TO 6

EGG WASH

1 large egg

¾ cup whole or 2% milk

1 tablespoon kosher salt

½ teaspoon freshly ground black pepper

½ teaspoon ground white pepper

2 cups all-purpose flour

One 3½- to 4-pound chicken, cut into 9 bone-in serving pieces

Vegetable oil, for frying

Back in 1878, the small settlement of Buffalo Gap was designated the Taylor County seat to honor three local Taylor brothers who fought at the Alamo. When the railroad was built in the 1880s, it bypassed Buffalo Gap and a new city, to be called Abilene after the Kansas cattle town, was planned along the train route. As Abilene grew into a shipping center, its citizens began to agitate to become the county seat. Two judges, one from each town, were to sort out the governmental matter. The Buffalo Gap judge ended up throwing his support behind Abilene. In retaliation, the local denizens raided the judge's property, absconded with his many chickens, and cooked up a fine fried chicken dinner. To hear people talk, you'd think this happened fifteen years ago, rather than fifteen decades ago. To honor this uprising, we serve fried chicken at every Sunday buffet.

1. To Make the Egg Wash: Whisk the egg in a shallow bowl. Add the milk, salt, black pepper, and white pepper and whisk until combined. Put the flour in another shallow bowl. Line a baking sheet with paper towels and set a wire baking rack on top.

2. Clip a deep-fry thermometer to the inside of a deep 12- or 14-inch cast-iron skillet or Dutch oven. Pour in oil to a depth of 3 inches and bring to 325°F over medium-high heat.

3. Dip the drumsticks in the egg wash, then dredge in the flour, shaking off any excess. Carefully lower them into the hot oil. Repeat with the wings, then the thighs, and then the breasts and the pulley bone, placing them skin side down in the oil. Fry for 15 minutes, then use tongs to turn each piece, using light pressure to avoid piercing the crust, and fry for an additional 15 to 17 minutes. To check for doneness, insert an instant-read thermometer into the meat of several pieces of chicken without touching the bone. The temperature should be 165°F and the crust should be a rich, golden brown on all sides, with the meat cooked through but still juicy. Drain the chicken on the wire rack. Serve hot.

Grill-Roasted Chicken Halves

SERVES 4 TO 6

2 chickens, about 3 to 3¼ pounds each

8 cups water

¼ cup plus 2 tablespoons granulated sugar

3 tablespoons kosher salt

6 tablespoons (¾ stick) unsalted butter, melted

3 tablespoons Perini Ranch Fish & Fowl Rub

Start this preparation a day before you plan to serve the chicken. After a night's brining, the halves get a slather of dry rub. This preparation comes out well on any grill, but if the fire is wood, as we use here at the Steakhouse, the flavor will be all the better.

1. The night before you plan to cook the chicken, begin preparations. Using kitchen scissors, cut each chicken in half down the back, cutting along each side of the backbone; discard the backbone. Cut the chicken in half on the breast side, cutting down along each side of the breastbone; discard the breastbone. Cut off the wing tips, the outermost wing joints. Press down on each chicken half's breast area with medium pressure. You're not trying to crush any bones, but simply flatten the chicken halves a bit for more even cooking.

2. In a large container, mix the water, sugar, and salt until the sugar and salt have dissolved. Immerse the chicken in the brine mixture, cover, and refrigerate overnight.

3. When ready to grill, remove the chicken from the refrigerator and drain the brine. Transfer the chicken to a baking sheet and pat dry using paper towels. Brush the chicken with butter on all sides. Rub the chicken gently with the dry rub, getting it both under and over the skin.

4. Fire up the grill, bringing the heat to medium (4 to 5 seconds with the hand test—see page 147).

5. Transfer the chicken halves, skin side down, to the cooking grate, stretching them out fully. Grill them uncovered for a total of 35 to 45 minutes, turning every 5 to 10 minutes. Toward the end of the grilling, turn the chicken skin side down for a final crisping. The chicken skin should face the grill long enough to render fat and brown gradually without burning.

Watch for flare-ups, shifting the chicken away from the flames as necessary. When the chicken halves are done, they will have crispy, golden brown skins, the legs will wiggle freely, and an instant-read thermometer inserted into the thickest portion of a thigh will register 170°F to 175°F.

6. Arrange the chicken more or less in a single layer on a platter, skin side up so the skin stays crisp. Serve right away.

Southern Fried Catfish with Tartar Sauce

Because we and other many of our customers are cattle ranchers, we don't offer much in the way of pork, seafood, or poultry, which are seen as competitors to the beef industry. The most notable exception is fried catfish, coated in spicy cornmeal and fried to golden crispness. It's nearly as popular at the Steakhouse and catering events as our steaks. In fact, we often serve catfish along with our Mesquite Smoked Peppered Beef Tenderloin as a second protein. Look for Mississippi farm-raised catfish which is consistently great and becomes flaky when cooked. Avoid imported or imitation catfish. Just about any of our sides go with fried catfish.

Credit for our homemade tartar sauce goes to our longtime manager Dale Cronk, who developed this recipe. Our catfish wouldn't be the same without it. It's chunky, fresh, and one of our most requested recipes.

SERVES 6

TARTAR SAUCE

1 cup mayonnaise

1 cup finely diced yellow onion

1 cup finely diced dill pickles, squeezed in paper towels to eliminate excess juice

1 tablespoon Worcestershire sauce

1 teaspoon Tabasco

½ teaspoon yellow mustard

½ teaspoon kosher salt, or more to taste

¼ teaspoon freshly ground black pepper

EGG WASH

1 large egg

¾ cup whole or 2% milk

2 teaspoons seasoned salt, such as Lawry's

½ teaspoon freshly ground white pepper

CORNMEAL COATING

2 cups medium-grind yellow cornmeal

¼ cup all-purpose flour

1 teaspoon kosher salt

1 teaspoon cayenne

½ teaspoon freshly ground black pepper

¼ teaspoon onion powder

¼ teaspoon garlic powder

Vegetable oil, for frying

Six 5- to 7-ounce catfish fillets, halved lengthwise if any are larger than others

1. To Make the Tartar Sauce: Whisk together all the ingredients in a bowl. Cover and refrigerate for up to 2 days, until ready to use.

2. To Make the Egg Wash: Whisk together all the ingredients in a shallow bowl.

3. **To Make the Coating:** Stir together all the ingredients in another shallow bowl.

4. **To Coat and Fry the Fish:** Clip a deep-fry thermometer to the inside of a deep 12- or 14-inch cast-iron skillet or Dutch oven. Pour in oil to a depth of 3 inches and bring to 325°F over medium-high heat. Line a baking sheet with paper towels. Put a wire baking rack on top of the paper towels.

Dip a catfish strip into the egg wash to coat and hold over the bowl for a few seconds so some of the egg wash drips off. Dredge it in the coating to cover well on all sides. Shake the strip to remove any excess coating, then carefully transfer to the hot oil. Repeat with another 6 strips. To maintain an even temperature, avoid crowding the skillet. Fry the strips for 5 to 6 minutes. When they are golden and float to the surface, place them on the wire rack. Repeat with the remaining strips. Serve hot with the tartar sauce.

Grilled Cajun Catfish

SERVES 4 TO 6

Vegetable oil spray

Six 8- to 10-ounce catfish fillets, each ¾ inch thick

3 medium limes, halved through their equators

2 tablespoons salted butter, melted

¼ cup Cajun seasoning

Tartar Sauce (page 184), for serving

An alternative to fried fish, this version is flaky with some crispiness to the edges.

1. Fire up the grill, bringing the temperature to medium-high (3 seconds with the hand test—see page 147). Mist a small-mesh grill rack with vegetable oil spray and place it over the grate.

2. Just before putting the fillets on the grill, spray both sides of each with vegetable oil spray, then spray the cut sides of each lime wedge. Arrange the limes around the edges of the grill. Place the fillets directly over the heat, drizzle lightly with about half the butter, and sprinkle evenly with half the Cajun seasoning. Grill the fillets uncovered for 3 minutes. Using a large spatula, carefully turn them, drizzle again with the remaining butter, sprinkle with the remaining Cajun seasoning, and cook for about 3 minutes. Carefully turn them once more, rotating a half-turn, so one side crisps a bit more than the other, and cook for a minute or two longer (for a total of 7 to 9 minutes).

3. Serve the fish immediately with a charred lime half and tartar sauce.

Grilled Whole Redfish

SERVES 2 TO 4

One 3-pound whole redfish or red snapper, deboned

2 to 3 tablespoons extra virgin olive oil

2 tablespoons Perini Ranch Fish & Fowl Rub

Orange or lemon halves, rubbed with more olive oil

A whole redfish, a mild, flaky, white Gulf fish, makes a striking presentation. Grill some orange or lemon halves, lightly basted with oil, beside it to add to the platter too.

1. Fire up the grill, bringing the temperature to medium-high (3 seconds with the hand test—see page 147).

2. Brush the fish inside and out with the oil, then massage with the dry rub.

3. Transfer the fish to a grill basket or a grill topper cooking grate. Grill for 8 to 9 minutes per inch of thickness. Turn the fish once after 4 to 5 minutes. Unless in a grill basket, gently roll the fish over its back side to flip it. The fish is ready when the flesh flakes easily. Add the citrus halves to the grill, cut side down, about the time you turn the fish, and let them cook long enough to get a bit of color. Arrange the fish and orange or lemon halves on a platter, and serve right away, squeezing the grilled citrus over the fish.

Shrimp and Sausage Gumbo

½ cup extra virgin olive oil

¾ cup all-purpose flour

2 cups chopped onion

2 cups chopped celery

2 cups chopped red bell pepper

2 cups chopped green bell pepper

2 garlic cloves, minced

1½ tablespoons Cajun seasoning

½ teaspoon ground black pepper

1½ pounds Cajun andouille or other lightly smoked pork sausage, sliced into thin half-moons

6 cups (1½ quarts) chicken stock

1 pound (26 to 30 per pound) peeled shrimp, left whole or halved lengthwise, if you wish

2 teaspoons file powder

White rice, for serving

A pot of gumbo's always a great one-dish meal for a football tailgate or other large casual get-together. Making the roux, or base, for it is the only tricky part. However, it just takes slow going and stirring to get the rich dark brown that helps flavor the mixture. You can make the base for it a day or some hours ahead, and add the shrimp just before serving.

John Montgomery, on our team, gets credit for this dish, but we hosted a pop-up dinner from the world-renowned Felix's Oyster Bar in New Orleans, and those great friends taught us how to make the roux. Sometime around Christmas, you can find John and Lisa out back taking turns stirring the roux.

1. In a Dutch oven or heavy stockpot, warm the oil over medium-high heat. Stir in the flour gradually, and continue to stir, making a deep reddish brown roux. This can take 20 or so minutes of nonstop stirring.

2. When the roux reaches the right color, immediately move the pot off the burner and stir in the onion, celery, and bell peppers. Return the pan to medium heat and cook for 3 to 4 minutes, until the vegetables have started to soften. Stir in the garlic, followed by the Cajun seasoning and pepper. Add the sausage and stock. Bring the mixture to a boil over medium-high heat, then reduce the heat as needed to simmer for 20 to 25 minutes, until the vegetables are tender and the flavors have melded.

3. Add the shrimp and file powder and heat through very briefly. Do not boil. Remove from heat and let the gumbo stand for about 15 minutes before serving in bowls over rice.

Dusted Fried Shrimp

SERVES 6

Vegetable oil, for frying

2 large eggs

¾ cup whole milk

1 teaspoon table salt

1¼ cups all-purpose flour

¼ cup Cajun seasoning

2½ pounds (16 to 20 per pound) shrimp, shelled, deveined, and tail-on

The secret to excellent fried shrimp is to keep the coating light and the oil hot (we use the term "dusted" to emphasize that our coating is light). The pink color of the shrimp should show through and you should be able to taste the shrimp as soon as you bite into the crackling, crisp crust. Enjoy with a squeeze of lemon, a favorite cocktail sauce, or perhaps our Remoulade (page 193).

1. Clip a deep-fry thermometer to the inside of a deep 12- or 14-inch cast-iron skillet or Dutch oven. Pour in oil to a depth of 3 inches and bring to 325°F over medium-high heat. Line a baking sheet with paper towels. Put a wire baking rack on top of the paper towels.

2. Whisk together the eggs, milk, and salt in a bowl. Combine the flour and Cajun seasoning in a shallow bowl. Add the shrimp to the egg mixture, stirring to coat all of them. One by one, dip the shrimp lightly in the flour mixture and shake to eliminate any excess flour. In batches, add the shrimp to the oil and fry until golden brown, about 1½ minutes. Don't crowd the pot or else the temperature of the oil will drop and the shrimp won't be crisp. When cooked, use a slotted spoon or tongs to transfer the shrimp to the wire rack. Repeat with the remaining shrimp. Serve hot.

Seafood Slaw

SERVES 6 OR MORE

REMOULADE

1 cup mayonnaise

2 tablespoons Creole mustard

2 tablespoons sweet pickle relish

1 tablespoon minced pickled jalapeño

1 tablespoon capers, drained

2 teaspoons minced fresh flat-leaf parsley leaves

1½ teaspoons Worcestershire sauce

½ teaspoon prepared horseradish

½ teaspoon anchovy paste

¼ teaspoon Old Bay seasoning

¼ teaspoon sweet paprika

SLAW

½ medium green cabbage, shredded

½ medium red cabbage, shredded

¼ cup salted pepitas (hulled pumpkin seeds)

1 pound (16 to 20 per pound) shrimp, cooked, peeled, deveined, and halved lengthwise

1 pound cooked lobster meat, cut into ½-inch pieces

Lisa created this as a cool summer catering entree, and we serve it plated or in martini glasses, depending on the occasion. The Louisiana-style remoulade really makes it.

1. To Make the Remoulade: Whisk together all the ingredients in a bowl. Makes 1½ cups. Cover and refrigerate for at least 1 hour or up to several days.

2. To Make the Slaw: Combine ½ cup of the remoulade, both cabbages, and the pepitas in a large bowl and toss well. Add the shrimp, lobster, and at least ½ cup remoulade and toss again. Refrigerate the slaw and remaining remoulade for at least 1 hour. Arrange the slaw on plates, drizzle with more remoulade if you wish, and serve.

SEAFOOD SALAD VARIATION: Skip the cabbage and pepitas: instead, mix the lobster and shrimp with a couple of diced celery stalks, about 1 cup halved seedless red grapes, and at least ½ cup of this creamy dressing: Mix together 1 scant cup mayonnaise, 1 heaping tablespoon minced fresh chives, ½ teaspoon lemon juice, and a good pinch each of salt and pepper. If you wish, serve each portion over a leaf of butter lettuce, and drizzle with any additional dressing.

Roasted Salmon with Tomato-Caper Relish

SERVES 6 TO 8

TOMATO-CAPER RELISH

8 to 10 ounces grape tomatoes, halved

1 medium shallot, thinly sliced

2 tablespoons drained capers

2 tablespoons red wine vinegar

¼ teaspoon kosher salt

One 2½- to 3-pound skin-on salmon fillet

¼ cup extra virgin olive oil

Kosher salt

1 to 2 tablespoons chopped fresh rosemary leaves

While we're all about beef at Perini Ranch Steakhouse, we do offer salmon with a colorful, Italian-inspired topping at parties we cater. The dish can be served warm or prepared ahead and served at room temperature or chilled.

1. To Start the Relish: Gently combine the tomatoes, shallot, capers, vinegar, and salt in a bowl. Let stand at room temperature for 30 minutes.

2. Heat the oven to 375°F. Arrange the salmon, skin side down, on a parchment paper–lined baking sheet. Brush the salmon with 2 tablespoons of the oil and sprinkle with the salt and rosemary.

3. Bake the salmon for 12 to 15 minutes, until lightly crisp on top and still somewhat translucent in the center when pierced with a knife.

4. While the salmon is baking, finish the relish: Heat the remaining 2 tablespoons olive oil in a skillet over medium heat. Stir in the tomato-caper mixture and sauté until the tomatoes are heated throughout and just limp, about 2 minutes. Set aside while the salmon finishes cooking.

5. The salmon can be served hot or at room temperature. Using a spatula, transfer the salmon to a platter and spoon the relish over the top.

Cacio e Pepe

SERVES 4

Kosher salt

1 pound spaghetti or bucatini

½ cup (1 stick) unsalted butter

1 tablespoon freshly ground black pepper

3 ounces (about 1½ cups lightly packed) Pecorino Romano cheese, grated on the fine holes of a box grater

1 ounce (about ½ cup lightly packed) Grana Padano or young Parmesan cheese, or additional Pecorino Romano cheese, grated on the fine holes of a box grater

If your name is Perini, you need to be able to whip up some great pasta. We love the simplicity of this preparation; with just a couple of key ingredients, you can create a decadent dish. We figure we've gravitated to this Roman dish partially because cracked black pepper, the *pepe* in the title, is a favorite ranch ingredient for flavoring our beef tenderloins as well as our cream gravy. Pecorino Romano, a sheep's milk cheese, traditionally flavors the pasta sauce. We like it combined with some cow's milk Grana Padano, made in the style of young Parmesan, which can be substituted. Use a good amount of starchy pasta cooking water to help create the silky sauce too. Because the ingredients are minimal, the technique is especially important here to avoid a gloppy sauce.

1. Bring a large pot of salted water to a boil over high heat. Add the pasta, give it a stir, and cook until very al dente, about 2 minutes less than the suggested cooking time on the package directions.

2. While the pasta is cooking, melt the butter in a large, heavy skillet over medium-low heat. Sauté the pepper in the butter for a couple of minutes, just until it is fragrant. Turn off the heat.

3. Before draining the pasta, scoop out 2 cups of the pasta water and reserve it. After draining the pasta, use tongs to transfer it to the skillet of butter and pepper. Warm the pasta over medium-low heat for a couple of minutes, twisting and turning it to coat all the pasta strands with butter. Add ½ cup of the pasta water to the skillet, then add one-half of each cheese to the pasta and keep twisting and turning it in the skillet to melt the cheese evenly and begin forming a creamy sauce. Resist turning up the heat to speed up the process. That's what clumps the cheese. Add another ½ cup pasta water followed by the rest of the cheese and keep stirring it together to coat each strand with the sauce. Pour in more of the pasta water as needed to produce a silky sauce. Taste and add a bit of salt, if needed. Serve immediately.

THE SIDE HUSTLE

Side dishes are almost a big a deal at the Steakhouse as beef. We have a pretty extensive list of possibilities, some that stay on the menu year-round, others that come and go with the seasons. Tom started with just a few options—the Green Chile Hominy, Zucchini Perini, the skillet-cooked Cowboy Potatoes. We now include a whole array of fresh vegetables and greens as well as beans and grits. Often, people find side dishes so good that they choose them as an entree. Tom frequently orders a Ranch Salad and a Zucchini Perini as his dinner. Help yourself!

Green Chile Hominy

SERVES 10 TO 12

Vegetable oil spray

10 slices bacon

1 cup chopped onion

Four 15-ounce cans white hominy, drained, with ½ cup liquid reserved

1 or 2 pickled jalapeños, minced, with 1 tablespoon liquid from the jar

1 cup chopped, roasted, peeled, and seeded New Mexico green or poblano chiles (page 219)

8 ounces (2 cups) shredded Cheddar cheese

If you only make one recipe from this book besides a steak, it should be this hominy. Not only is it a Steakhouse signature, on the menu from almost day one, but it works equally well for breakfast and dinner. Tom created the dish when working with the late Louise Matthews of Albany, Texas. Mrs. Matthews held an epic party in conjunction with the Fort Griffin Fandangle, the oldest outdoor musical production in Texas, which showcases ranching life in West Central Texas with music and merriment. You can assemble the hominy dish a day ahead.

1. Heat the oven to 350°F. Mist a 9x13-inch baking dish at least 2 inches deep with vegetable oil spray.

2. Put the bacon slices in a cold skillet. Turn the heat to medium-low and cook the bacon for 3 minutes on one side. Turn the bacon and cook on the other side to desired doneness. Remove the bacon with a slotted spoon and drain on paper towels. When cool enough to handle, crumble the bacon with your fingers and set aside.

3. Carefully pour off all but 2 to 3 tablespoons of the bacon drippings. Return the skillet to the stovetop and stir in the onion. Cook over medium heat until the onion is tender, 5 minutes.

4. Pour in the hominy liquid and jalapeño liquid and cook until reduced by about one-half, about 5 minutes. Add the hominy and jalapeños and heat through. Stir in half of the crumbled bacon and half of the cheese.

5. Spoon into the prepared baking dish. Scatter the remaining bacon and cheese over the hominy. Bake for 25 minutes, until the cheese on top melts and the hominy mixture is bubbly. Let sit for 5 minutes before serving.

Zucchini Perini

SERVES 6 TO 8

½ pound ground beef

½ pound ground Italian pork sausage, preferably hot

1 large onion, finely diced

One 28-ounce can whole tomatoes, drained and cut into pieces

One 6-ounce can tomato paste

¼ cup tomato sauce

2 teaspoons crumbled dried oregano

⅛ teaspoon garlic powder

2 pounds zucchini, sliced into ¼-inch-thick rounds

Kosher salt and freshly ground black pepper

¼ cup grated Parmesan cheese

½ cup toasted panko (page 236)

2½ tablespoons dried parsley

Has a nice ring to it, doesn't it? We think the smile the name brings gets some folks who might otherwise skip over vegetables to give it a try. Since zucchini grows like—well, zucchini—in Texas in the warm months, it's really handy to have a good recipe to use them up. Turn your head for a minute, and those petite hand-size zukes turn into baseball bats.

1. Heat the oven to 350°F. In a large, oven-safe skillet, sauté the ground beef, sausage, and onion over medium-high heat until the meat is evenly browned and the onion is limp, 5 to 8 minutes. Stir in the tomatoes, tomato paste, and tomato sauce and mix well. Stir in the oregano and garlic powder. Reduce the heat to medium and simmer for 5 minutes. Stir in the zucchini and season with salt and pepper. Continue cooking just until the zucchini wilts, about 5 minutes. Sprinkle the Parmesan on top.

2. Transfer the skillet to the oven and bake for 10 to 12 minutes, until the zucchini is fork-tender and the cheese has melted and browned in spots. Remove from the oven. Combine the panko and parsley and scatter the mixture evenly over the zucchini. Let sit for 5 minutes before serving.

Old-Fashioned Green Beans

SERVES 6 TO 8

Two 28-ounce cans Allens Seasoned Cut Italian Green Beans or other canned cut Italian green beans

⅔ cup minced white onion

1½ to 2 tablespoons bacon drippings or vegetable oil

½ teaspoon freshly ground black pepper

Kosher salt

Old-fashioned green beans generally are long-cooked to delectable tenderness with seasonings such as bacon drippings and a good hit of black pepper. We start with already tender canned Italian-style green beans, then add more zip to them.

1. Combine the beans and their liquid, onion, bacon drippings, and pepper in a large saucepan. Bring to a boil, then reduce to a simmer and cook about 10 minutes, until the onion is tender. Season with salt to taste.

2. Turn off the heat and let the beans sit for 15 minutes for the flavors to meld. Reheat if you wish, and serve the beans in small bowls with some of the juices.

BACON DRIPPINGS

Up until a generation ago, cooks kept an old coffee can or small crock of bacon drippings, poured off from the cast-iron skillet from frying each morning's bacon. No one ever refrigerated the drippings back in the day. They were just kept under the sink or on top of the stove to be used to grease the skillet for cornbread, vegetables, and chicken-fried steak. Drippings were considered liquid gold, a kitchen gift that just kept on giving.

If you want to save the flavorful fat, keep it in the fridge to make sure it doesn't spoil. Some folks go to the effort of straining the drippings when pouring them into the storage container, but we don't bother. There are always bacon drippings in our home fridge.

Grilled Asparagus

SERVES 6

1½ pounds asparagus spears, preferably medium-thick, trimmed of tough ends

Extra virgin olive oil

Kosher salt and freshly ground black pepper

One of the best practical jokes ever played on Tom was by Mario Espino, our ranch manager of more than twenty years. Tom had been nursing along a bed of asparagus in our Steakhouse garden. Some of you will know that asparagus takes about three years to root and shoot up, in a quantity that amounts to a meal. Tom was really excited by year three, checking the bed once or twice a day, ready to harvest his first crop. One morning, dozens of asparagus spears had shot up overnight. Why, they were 6, 8, 10 inches tall! Lisa was back at the house and got a call: "Get down here now. The asparagus has done it!" There was much marveling at the crop, though it started to sink in that it looked just a tad too perfect. When Tom went closer to investigate, he discovered that Mario had stuck a whole passel of grocery store asparagus into the ground overnight.

1. Fire up the grill, bringing the temperature to medium (4 to 5 seconds with the hand test—see page 147). For the best flavor if cooking over gas or charcoal, add a half-dozen mesquite chunks to the fire a few minutes before placing the asparagus on the grill.

2. Toss the asparagus in a shallow baking dish with enough oil to coat lightly. Sprinkle with salt and pepper. Transfer the asparagus to the grill, perpendicular to the cooking grate and placing the stems over the hottest part of the fire and the tips toward an outer edge. Grill uncovered for 5 to 8 minutes, depending on the thickness, rolling them frequently to cook on all sides. Serve warm or at room temperature, perhaps with another drizzle of oil and an extra sprinkling of salt and pepper.

Fried Okra

SERVES 6 OR MORE

1½ pounds small okra, sliced into ½-inch-thick rings

2 teaspoons kosher salt

Vegetable oil, for pan-frying

1 cup all-purpose flour

1 cup dry bread crumbs

1 teaspoon granulated garlic

1 teaspoon celery salt

1 teaspoon freshly ground black pepper

Every true Southerner loves okra, and frying is the best method of cooking this vegetable. Fried okra should be delectably crunchy, almost like popcorn.

1. In a bowl, cover the okra with ice water and stir in 1 teaspoon salt to keep the okra crisp. Let the okra soak at room temperature for 15 to 30 minutes.

2. Clip a deep-fry thermometer to the inside of a deep 12- or 14-inch cast-iron skillet or Dutch oven. Pour in oil to a depth 1½ to 2 inches and bring to 325°F over medium-high heat. Line a baking sheet with paper towels. Put a wire baking rack on top of the paper towels.

3. Combine the flour, bread crumbs, granulated garlic, celery salt, remaining 1 teaspoon salt, and the pepper on a shallow plate.

4. Drain the okra in a colander, but do not dry completely. Coat the damp okra with the breading, then transfer to a strainer and shake off any excess. Using a large slotted spoon, lower about one-half of the okra into the hot oil. Don't overcrowd the skillet. Fry the okra just until golden, 1 to 2 minutes. Stir occasionally to fry evenly. Drain the okra on the wire rack. Continue to fry the remaining okra. Serve hot.

Creamed Spinach

3 tablespoons unsalted butter

½ cup minced white or yellow onion

1 garlic clove, minced

2 pounds thawed frozen chopped spinach

3 ounces cream cheese, cut in 6 cubes

1 cup heavy cream

1¼ teaspoons kosher salt

1 teaspoon fresh ground black pepper

⅛ teaspoon ground nutmeg

We often offer creamed spinach on the Steakhouse menu. It's a seasonal dish, not always on the menu, but when it is, you can count on Lisa ordering it. The cream cheese included gives it a nice mild tang.

1. Melt the butter in a saucepan over medium heat. Stir in the onion and garlic and cook until soft and translucent, about 3 minutes.

2. Drain any standing watery liquid from the spinach. Add the spinach to the pan and stir up from the bottom. Cook for about 5 minutes, until most liquid from the spinach has evaporated.

3. Add in the cream cheese, giving it a stir, then pour in the cream. Simmer for 10 to 15 minutes, stirring frequently to avoid scorching, until the spinach is quite tender and the cream thickened and reduced. Serve hot.

A Mess of Greens
with Potlikker

SERVES 8

1 pound fresh collard greens

1 pound fresh mustard greens

1 pound fresh turnip greens

4 cups low-sodium chicken stock

¾ teaspoon kosher salt

¾ teaspoon freshly ground black pepper

Tabasco or other hot pepper sauce

If you didn't grow up somewhere between Texas and South Carolina, you may not know that the term "mess" refers—in Southern food terms—to a large batch of something, most often greens. These three voluminous greens (collard, mustard, and turnip) all wilt down substantially during cooking. The liquid in which greens or other vegetables are simmered is called "potlikker," a magical elixir full of vitamins from the greens cooked in it. You just might catch Tom in the kitchen, dunking a coffee mug into the greens for a little of the potlikker.

1. Cut off the greens' stem ends from the leaves. Chop the leaves of the greens into 3-inch pieces.

2. Combine the stock, 4 cups of water, salt, and pepper in a large pot and bring to a boil over high heat. Add the greens to the pot, pushing them down into the liquid with a large spoon. Cover and reduce the heat to medium. Cook the greens for at least 20 minutes, stirring occasionally. (If the liquid evaporates, add some more water or stock. The greens should always be submerged.) Pierce the greens with a fork to check for tenderness. For softer greens, cook for an additional 10 minutes. Serve the greens spooned out into bowls with some of the potlikker. Pass the hot pepper sauce at the table.

Spicy Brussels Sprouts

SERVES 6

2 pounds Brussels sprouts, trimmed and halved

2 tablespoons extra virgin olive oil

1½ teaspoons kosher salt

½ teaspoon red pepper flakes, or more to taste

When you add a little zip to this sometimes plain Jane vegetable, it turns into a star of dinner. People sometimes ask for a double order.

1. Heat the oven to 350°F.

2. Toss the Brussels sprouts in a bowl with the remaining ingredients. Transfer to a baking sheet in a single layer. Bake for about 20 minutes, until tender with a few brown edges. Enjoy right away.

TOM'S TIP: We sometimes add thin strips of red bell pepper to the Brussels sprouts to give a little more color to the dish. Use about half of a large red bell pepper, and bake the strips along with the sprouts.

Yellow Squash Casserole

SERVES 6 TO 8

¼ cup (½ stick) salted butter, at room temperature

1 large sweet onion, halved from top to bottom, then sliced ⅛ inch thick, preferably on a mandoline

2 large eggs, beaten

¼ cup whole milk

1 teaspoon kosher salt

½ teaspoon freshly ground black pepper

2½ pounds yellow summer squash, sliced ¼ inch thick, preferably on a mandoline

2½ cups (10 ounces) shredded medium or sharp Cheddar cheese

½ cup panko, toasted in a dry skillet

½ cup chopped fresh basil leaves

Nothing is more exciting to a gardener than the first picking of tiny, tender yellow squash. Nothing is less exciting than the 98th picking of that same squash. Here's the traditional Texas way of smothering summer squash (or other vegetables) in casseroles with cheese, but the fresh basil makes it especially wonderful. It's as delicious as it is popular.

1. Heat the oven to 375°F. Grease a 9x13-inch baking dish with 1 tablespoon of the butter.

2. Melt the remaining 3 tablespoons of butter in a large skillet over medium heat. Stir in the onion and sauté until tender and translucent. Cool briefly.

3. Whisk together the eggs, milk, salt, and pepper in a large bowl. Stir in the cooked onion, squash, 2 cups of the Cheddar, half of the panko, and half of the basil. Spoon the mixture into the baking dish. Scatter the remaining ½ cup Cheddar, ¼ cup panko, and ¼ cup basil over the squash mixture. Cover the casserole with aluminum foil.

4. Bake for 30 minutes. Remove the foil and continue baking for an additional 15 minutes, until the squash is tender and the casserole is bubbly. Let sit for 5 to 10 minutes before serving.

Bourbon-Glazed Carrots

SERVES 6

1 pound baby carrots

½ teaspoon kosher salt, plus more to taste

¼ cup packed brown sugar

¼ teaspoon ground cinnamon

Pinch or 2 cayenne

¼ cup coarsely chopped pecans

¼ cup (½ stick) salted butter, cut into small pieces

2 tablespoons bourbon

You want to get a cowboy—or just about anyone else—to eat a vegetable? Cover it in bourbon and brown sugar. Luckily that's a winning combination when it comes to carrots. We use Maker's Mark, but any bourbon you drink is fine.

1. Bring a medium saucepan of water to a boil. Add the carrots and salt, reduce the heat to a simmer, and cook for 8 to 10 minutes, until the carrots can just be pierced with a fork. Drain in a colander and return the carrots to the pan.

2. While the carrots are cooking, stir together the brown sugar, cinnamon, and cayenne in a bowl. Toast the pecans in a dry skillet over medium-low heat, stirring often so they don't burn, until they are aromatic. Set aside.

3. Stir the butter into the warm carrots and return to low heat. When melted, add the bourbon, then stir in the brown sugar mixture. Continue cooking, stirring frequently, until the carrots are glazed and tender. Add salt to taste. Top the glazed carrots with the pecans and serve.

Mesquite Grilled Eggplant Parmesan

SERVES 8

2 tablespoons extra virgin olive oil, plus more for the eggplant and the baking dish

½ cup diced onion

2 garlic cloves, minced

One 28-ounce can whole peeled tomatoes, such as Cento brand

1½ teaspoons crumbled dried oregano

½ teaspoon red pepper flakes

1 large eggplant, cut into ¼-inch-thick slices

1 teaspoon kosher salt

1 teaspoon freshly ground black pepper

8 ounces mozzarella cheese, cubed

½ cup thinly sliced fresh basil leaves

½ cup panko

½ cup grated Parmesan cheese

Lots of eggplant Parmesan recipes call for breading and frying the eggplant before assembling the casserole. But we found that grilling the eggplant slices makes them tender rather than heavy, adds a note of rusticity from the mesquite coals' light smoke, and makes this recipe unique to Perini Ranch. While traveling in Italy, we took a cooking class that featured eggplant Parmesan. We're more convinced than ever that mesquite-grilling the eggplant is the way to go. This dish is a great blend of Tom's Italian heritage and real Texas cooking.

1. Heat the oven to 400°F. Warm the oil in a medium saucepan over medium heat. Stir in the onion and garlic. Cook, stirring frequently, until the onions are tender. Add the tomatoes, cutting them up with a spoon or crushing them with your fingers as they go into the pan. Stir in the oregano and red pepper flakes. Simmer the sauce for 10 minutes to thicken.

2. Fire up the grill, bringing the temperature to medium (4 to 5 seconds with the hand test—see page 147). For the best flavor if cooking over gas or charcoal, add a half-dozen mesquite chunks to the fire a few minutes before placing the eggplant on the grill.

3. Lightly brush the eggplant slices with olive oil and season with salt and pepper. Grill the eggplant slices about 4 minutes per side, until limp. They will cook further when baked.

4. Brush a 9 x 13-inch baking dish with olive oil. Spread 1 cup tomato sauce in the bottom of the dish. Top with about one-third of the eggplant, followed by half of the mozzarella and half of the basil. Repeat with the tomato sauce, eggplant, mozzarella, and basil. Top the second layer with the remaining eggplant and tomato sauce. Evenly sprinkle the panko and Parmesan on top. Bake for 30 minutes, until heated through and bubbly on top. Increase the oven temperature to 500°F and bake for an additional 5 minutes to brown the top. Let sit for 5 to 10 minutes before serving.

Fire-Roasted Vegetables

SERVES 6 OR MORE

½ cup extra virgin olive oil

½ teaspoon kosher salt

¼ teaspoon freshly ground black pepper

VEGETABLES

1 large red onion, cut into ⅓-inch-thick rounds

1 large sweet onion, cut into ⅓-inch-thick rounds

8 ounces small mushroom caps

1 medium eggplant, cut into ½-inch-thick rounds

3 or 4 red or yellow bell peppers, halved and seeded

3 or 4 New Mexico green or poblano chiles, halved and seeded

Green onions, any limp green tops cut off

1 or 2 zucchini or yellow squash, cut lengthwise into ½-inch-thick pieces

2 sweet potatoes, peeled and cut into ⅓-inch-thick rounds

Vegetable oil spray

Francis Mallmann, the visionary Argentinian chef, was our guest at the three-day 2014 Buffalo Gap Wine & Food Summit. Francis has a collection of techniques for cooking with wood and coals that he details in his book *Seven Fires*. For his visit, we fabricated all seven fires, which included a variety of grills, cooking surfaces, and iron baskets for burning wood down to coals. Our ranch crew dug trenches and pits. It was a hazy, smoke-tinged, other-worldly scene for days.

But unless you're already planning to cook a few lambs, sides of beef, or massively large fish and expect to have loads of hot ash, we figured a simple grilling of smaller vegetable slices will serve you better. We just love the earthy flavors and colors grill-roasted vegetables bring to the plate. Pick out four or five of the vegetables listed and make a big platter.

You can use metal or bamboo skewers for the onions. If using bamboo, soak them in water for 20 minutes so they don't burn on the grill.

1. Whisk the oil, salt, and pepper together in a bowl.

2. Fire up the grill, bringing the temperature to medium (4 to 5 seconds with the hand test—see page 147). For the best flavor if cooking over gas or charcoal, add a half-dozen mesquite chunks to the fire a few minutes before grilling. Thread skewers through the red and sweet onion slices. Mist all of the vegetables on all sides with vegetable oil spray.

3. Grill the vegetables, uncovered, over medium heat, rotating them a half turn each time for grill marks and scattering on the salt as they cook on each side, until tender. This will take 8 to 10 minutes for the mushroom caps; 10 to 12 minutes for the eggplant, peppers, chiles, and green onions; 12 to 15 minutes for the zucchini or yellow squash; and 18 to 20 minutes for the sweet potatoes and onion slices, turning all of them twice on each side. As the vegetables finish, transfer them to a platter. Slide the onions off the skewers and pull any loose skins from the bell peppers and chiles and thinly slice. Drizzle with the seasoned oil, as desired, and serve.

Roasted Corn on the Cob with Chile-Lime Butter

SERVES 6 OR MORE

CHILE-LIME BUTTER

1 cup (2 sticks) salted butter

Juice of 1 lime

Pinch of cayenne

6 to 8 fresh ears of corn

Kosher salt and freshly ground black pepper

Is there anything that says summer as emphatically and deliciously as corn on the cob? Cooking ears in their husks over the grill adds an extra touch of showmanship and flavor.

1. Fire up the grill, bringing the temperature to medium (4 to 5 seconds with the hand test—see page 147). For the best flavor if cooking over gas or charcoal, add a half-dozen mesquite chunks to the fire a few minutes before grilling the corn.

2. To Make the Chile-Lime Butter: Melt the butter with the lime juice and cayenne in a wide, shallow pan (for rolling the ears of corn). Once melted, keep the butter warm.

3. To Roast the Corn: Remove all but the last 3 or 4 husks from each ear of corn but keep them attached at the end. The corn silks will dry while the corn is on the grill and will easily pull away from the cobs. (Save several of the longer, stronger husks and shred into ½-inch strips to tie back the other husks on the cooked ears of corn.) Put the corn on the grill and cook, turning on all sides with tongs for a total of 8 to 10 minutes. When done, the corn kernels should be tender but still a bit firm when pierced with a fork, and kissed with flecks of brown from the fire. Wearing mitts, pull back the husks and discard the silks. Tie back the husks that remain on each cob with the strips of reserved corn husk.

4. Using tongs, roll each hot ear of corn in the warm butter. Offer salt and pepper at the table. Serve hot with plenty of napkins.

Roasted Corn and Poblano Pudding

SERVES 8

Vegetable oil spray

6 thick slices bacon

¾ cup (1½ sticks) unsalted butter

¾ cup chopped onion

½ teaspoon kosher salt

½ teaspoon freshly ground black pepper

2 poblano chiles, roasted, peeled, seeded, and diced (opposite page)

5 cups grill-roasted corn kernels (from 5 ears; page 217)

¾ cup heavy whipping cream

One 8-ounce package cream cheese, cut into cubes, at room temperature

¾ cup grated Parmesan cheese

3 large eggs

⅓ cup whole milk

Corn and chiles go together like tequila and limes. A poblano is a fresh green chile similar in heat to the New Mexico green chile. The deeper green poblanos take their name from the Mexican city of Puebla and are distinguished by their broad "shoulders." The flavor is a bit earthier than the slimmer New Mexico chile pods. This recipe is decadent, rich, and almost a meal by itself. While it's one of our newer menu additions, this side already has a huge following. Many have requested this recipe—here it is!

1. Heat the oven to 350°F. Mist a 9x13-inch baking dish with vegetable oil spray.

2. Put the bacon slices in a large, cold skillet. Turn the heat to medium-low and cook the bacon for 3 minutes on one side. Turn the bacon and cook on the other side to desired doneness. Remove the bacon with a slotted spoon and drain on paper towels. When cool enough to handle, crumble the bacon with your fingers and set aside. Discard all but 2 tablespoons of the bacon fat.

3. Add the butter, onion, salt, and pepper to the bacon drippings in the skillet and cook over medium heat until the onions are soft. Add the poblanos, corn, cream, cream cheese, and Parmesan, stirring well to combine.

4. Whisk together the eggs and milk in a bowl. Add about ½ cup of the hot corn mixture to the eggs, so the eggs won't scramble. Add the egg mixture to the corn mixture and stir well. Pour the corn mixture into the prepared dish and stir in the bacon. Cover with aluminum foil and bake for 45 minutes. Uncover and bake for an additional 10 minutes, until the top browns. Let sit for 10 minutes before serving.

ROASTING AND PEELING GREEN CHILES

Chiles and peppers are best when they are roasted and their skins are removed. This can easily be done in an oven, on top of a gas stove, or on an outdoor grill.

To roast in the oven, heat the oven to 450°F. Arrange the chiles in a single layer on a baking sheet and roast until blistered and blackened on all sides, turning them as necessary until they collapse.

If you are roasting only a couple of chiles or peppers, use tongs and hold them over the flame of a gas burner for a few minutes, until they blacken on all sides.

Chiles and peppers can also be roasted on the grate of a charcoal, gas, or wood-burning grill. Sear on all sides for 10 minutes.

Once the chiles or peppers are roasted, immediately place them in a plastic bag and seal, or place in a bowl and cover with foil. Let them sit for 5 to 10 minutes, or until cool enough to handle. Put on disposable gloves if dealing with chiles. This is to avoid getting capsaicin, the substance that gives chiles their heat, on your hands. It doesn't wash off easily and can irritate the skin. Using your gloved fingers, strip off the skins. If a bit of blackened skin remains, that's fine. Avoid running water over the chiles, because their flavor will become diluted. Remove the stems and seeds and slice or chop the chiles as needed.

Cowboy Potatoes

SERVES 8 OR MORE

4 pounds red waxy potatoes such as Red Bliss, cut into thick wedges

½ cup (1 stick) salted butter, melted

1 medium white onion, thinly sliced

1 or 2 garlic cloves, minced

1 teaspoon kosher salt

1 teaspoon freshly ground black pepper

½ teaspoon crumbled dried oregano

Here's the side dish most popular with our cowboys and ranchers—kind of elemental in its preparation and in its appeal. For a buffet, serve them up in a hefty cast-iron skillet. Nothing beats these when it comes to a steak-and-potato meal.

1. Heat the oven to 350°F. In a large shallow bowl, toss together the potato wedges, butter, onion, garlic, salt, pepper, and oregano. Spoon into a shallow baking dish and cover with aluminum foil.

2. Bake for 1 hour, stirring occasionally. Remove the foil and continue baking for another 30 minutes. The potatoes should be lightly crusted in spots and tender when pierced with a fork. Let rest for 5 to 10 minutes before serving.

TOM'S TIP: We sure never mind having leftover Cowboy Potatoes. They can be topped with an egg for breakfast, added to an omelet or frittata, or become the filling for burritos, tacos, and more. They're a gift that keeps on giving.

Mashed Potatoes

SERVES 6 TO 8

3 pounds russet or other large baking potatoes

1½ tablespoons kosher salt, or more to taste

¾ cup (1½ sticks) salted butter

¾ cup heavy cream

¾ teaspoon freshly ground black pepper

If there isn't a Texas state law requiring that mashed potatoes be served with chicken-fried steak and fried chicken (often referred to around these parts as chicken-fried chicken) and topped with some cream gravy, there ought to be. Ours are classic with a bit of a rustic look, because we leave on some of the peel and mash them by hand so there are some small potato chunks. Of course, mashed potatoes can accompany just about anything—grilled steak, braised short ribs, or fried chicken.

1. Wash the potatoes and partially peel them, leaving about half of the peels in place, then cut into 2-inch chunks. Combine them in a large pot with enough water to cover by at least an inch, then add the salt. Bring to a boil over high heat, then reduce the heat to medium and cook until quite tender, 15 to 20 minutes. When done, the exteriors of the potato chunks should be crumbly, almost dissolving in spots.

2. While the potatoes cook, heat the butter and cream together in a saucepan, just until bubbles form around the edge.

3. Drain the potatoes, then return to the warm pot. Drizzle in the warm butter-cream mixture, mashing the potatoes with a potato masher as you go. Leave a few small chunks of potato. Season with pepper and, if you wish, more salt. Serve piping hot.

BLUE CHEESE MASHED POTATOES: Prepare the potatoes as above, using only 1½ teaspoons salt in the cooking water. When you add the cream-butter mixture, stir in ½ to ¾ cup room-temperature blue cheese crumbles, preferably a mild Danish blue cheese. Taste for seasoning and serve.

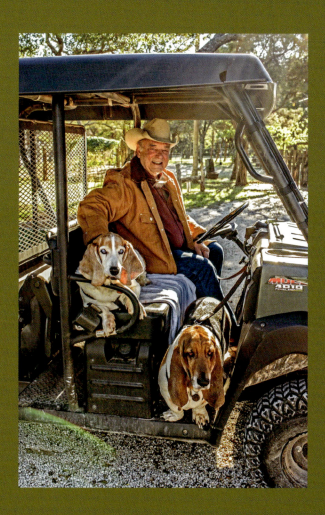

OUR FOUR-LEGGED AMBASSADORS

When you think of a ranch dog, the basset hound—with its short legs, long ears, and an even longer body—probably doesn't come to mind. Lisa brought the first basset hound into our lives. That was Gus, who even wrote his own book, *Tails of Perini Ranch*, about all the cool things to do around the property. Gus was lucky enough to have Miss Beazley, a former White House dog, pen the foreword to his book. Miss Beazley noted that she had dictated her words to a member of *her* staff, Laura Bush, and to please excuse any typos that Mrs. Bush might have made.

The late Gus was named after Captain Augustus "Gus" McCrae, a character from Larry McMurtry's seminal western novel, *Lonesome Dove*. Our friend Robert Duvall played Gus in the memorable TV mini-series. Gus's younger brother, Jett, was the namesake of Jett Rink, the character James Dean played in the movie *Giant*. Today, Jett is top dog, with two younger brothers, Winston and Oliver. The three of them, ears a-flapping, check out the ranch with Tom, riding in his "mule," a four-wheeled heavy-duty open-sided vehicle. Daily at 8:00 a.m., Tom, Jett, Winston, and Oliver load up in the mule and head to the Steakhouse for coffee and the morning meeting to plan the day.

Twice-Baked Potato Casserole

SERVES 8

¼ cup (½ stick) salted butter, melted, plus more for the baking dish

2 pounds russet potatoes

2 or 3 thick slices bacon

1 cup (4 ounces) shredded Cheddar cheese

2 ounces cream cheese, at room temperature

8 ounces sour cream

¼ cup whole milk

1 garlic clove, minced

¾ teaspoon kosher salt

½ teaspoon freshly ground black pepper

½ cup thinly sliced green onion tops, light and dark green portions

W̲e don't serve baked potatoes or French fries at the Steakhouse. When Tom opened the Steakhouse, he was committed to offering unique sides, like Green Chile Hominy (page 199) and Zucchini Perini (page 200). We like to think our sides are as popular and crowd pleasing as our entrees. This potato casserole has all the baked potato toppings, so no decisions need to be made.

1. Heat the oven to 375°F. Butter a 9x13-inch baking dish at least 2 inches deep.

2. Use a fork to prick a few holes in each potato. Put the potatoes directly on the center oven rack. Bake for 45 to 60 minutes (depending on their size), until they can easily be pierced with a fork.

3. While the potatoes are baking, cook the bacon: Put the bacon slices in a cold skillet. Turn the heat to medium-low and cook the bacon for 3 minutes on one side. Turn the bacon and cook on the other side to desired doneness. Remove the bacon with a slotted spoon and drain on paper towels. When cool enough to handle, use your hands to break the bacon into small pieces.

4. Remove the potatoes, leaving the oven on. When the potatoes are cool enough to handle, cut them in half and scoop out the flesh into a bowl. Using a potato masher, mash the potatoes well. Stir in the Cheddar, cream cheese, sour cream, milk, and butter. Mix in the bacon, garlic, salt, pepper, and ¼ cup of the green onions.

5. Evenly spoon the mixture into the baking dish. Bake for 30 to 35 minutes, until heated through and bubbly. Let rest for 5 to 10 minutes. Scatter the remaining ¼ cup green onions on top before serving.

Au Gratin Potatoes

SERVES 6

1 cup heavy cream

¼ cup (½ stick) salted butter

1½ teaspoons table salt

1½ teaspoons freshly ground black pepper

1½ teaspoons granulated garlic

2 pounds red potatoes, sliced ¼-inch thick

½ large onion, sliced thinly, julienne style

1 cup (about 4 ounces) grated Parmesan cheese

Vegetable oil spray

As you've seen, we whip up a lot of potato dishes. They are good "keepers," if you're out on the range. They're also filling, satisfying, and relatively inexpensive. And what's better with butter, cream, and cheese?

1. Heat the oven to 350°F. Butter a 9x13-inch baking dish. In a large saucepan, warm the cream and butter over medium heat until the butter melts. Stir in the salt, pepper, and garlic. Add the potatoes and onion and mix together to coat with the cream mixture. Remove from the heat. Mix in half of the Parmesan cheese.

2. Spoon the potato mixture into the prepared dish. Sprinkle with the remaining Parmesan. Mist a piece of foil large enough to cover the potatoes with vegetable oil spray, then cover them.

3. Bake for about 50 minutes, until the potatoes are tender. Uncover and continue baking for 5 to 10 minutes more, until the top colors a bit. Serve.

Matty's Potato and Sweet Potato Gratin

SERVES 6

1 pound sweet potatoes, peeled and sliced ⅛-inch thick

1 pound Yukon Gold potatoes, peeled and sliced ⅛-inch thick

3 cups (about 12 ounces) grated Gruyère cheese

1 tablespoon minced fresh rosemary

1 teaspoon table salt

½ teaspoon freshly ground black pepper

2 teaspoons minced garlic

2 cups heavy cream

Vegetable oil spray

We mentioned our chef friend Matthew Wendel under the Country Potato Salad recipe. The guy has quite a way with potatoes. These rosemary and Gruyère–flavored ones, combined with sweet potatoes, also were inspired by Matty, as he's known. He created a version of this dish while working for President George W. Bush and First Lady Laura Bush. Matty's book, *Recipes from the President's Ranch* (The White House Historical Association, 2020) is a favorite of ours.

1. Heat the oven to 350°F. Butter a 9x13-inch baking dish. Make a layer from about half of the sweet potato slices, and scatter with about ½ cup of cheese and about one-third of the rosemary, salt, and pepper. Make a layer of Yukon Gold potatoes. Scatter with about ½ cup more cheese and another one-third of the rosemary, salt, and pepper. Repeat with another layer of sweet potatoes, cheese, rosemary, salt, and pepper. Add a top layer of potatoes. Stir the garlic into the cream and pour it evenly over the potato mixture. Top with the remaining cheese.

2. Mist a piece of foil large enough to cover the dish with vegetable oil spray. Cover the dish with the foil. Bake for 45 minutes. Uncover and bake for about 15 additional minutes, or until potatoes and sweet potatoes are tender and the cheese topping lightly browned. Let stand for 10 to 15 minutes before serving.

Honest-to-Goodness
French Fries

SERVES 6

4 large russet or other baking potatoes, each about ¾ pound

Several handfuls ice cubes

Peanut oil or vegetable oil, for frying

1 tablespoon table salt, or more to taste

FRIED JALAPEÑOS

¾ cup all-purpose flour

2 teaspoons Cajun seasoning

½ cup pickled jalapeño slices, drained but still moist

With the proliferation of French fries at fast-food establishments everywhere, it might not occur to you to make your own. For genuinely world-class fries, worthy of a special occasion, cook your own this way. You'll be frying them twice. To give them a bit more Perini pizzazz, we toss them at the end with some fried jalapeño. People go crazy for them with the burgers and sandwiches at The Gap Café.

1. To Make the French Fries: Fill a large bowl with very cold water. Peel the potatoes and slice them lengthwise into fat matchsticks, about ⅜ inch thick. (An inexpensive V-slicer makes easy work of this.) Toss the potatoes into the bowl of water as they are cut. Once all of the potatoes are in the bowl, pour off the water to eliminate some of the starch. Add more cold water to cover and put the ice cubes in the bowl. Place the bowl in the refrigerator and let the potatoes soak for at least 30 minutes and up to overnight, to crisp them and eliminate more starch. Pour off the water again, then spread out the potatoes on clean dish towels to dry. You can also dry the potatoes in batches in a salad spinner.

You will be frying the potatoes twice. Up to 1 hour before you plan to eat, fry the potatoes for the first time. Pour 4 to 5 inches of oil into a large heavy pot suitable for deep-frying and heat the oil to 280°F. Arrange a large baking rack over several thick layers of paper towels on a baking sheet. Add the potatoes to the pot in batches and par-fry them for about for 5 to 8 minutes, until they are soft and they have gone from opaque white to semi-translucent. Limp and pale, they will look rather unpromising. Remove them with a skimmer or spider strainer, preferably, or large slotted spoon. Spread them on the baking rack. Turn off the heat under the oil. Let the fries rest for at least 15 minutes and up to an hour.

2. To Make the Fried Jalapeños: While the fries are resting, combine the flour and Cajun seasoning in a medium bowl. Toss the jalapeños with the flour mixture and reserve.

Just before serving, reheat the oil, this time to 350°F. Fry the potatoes in batches again, this time for 2 to 4 minutes each, or until they are crispy and golden brown. Remove them with a skimmer or spider and drain. Toss immediately with the salt, then transfer to a large platter. The fries will retain more crispness if spread out rather than piled high. Immediately fry the jalapeños in the oil for about 1 minute, until the flour coating is crisp. Drain them and toss them with the fries. Serve piping hot.

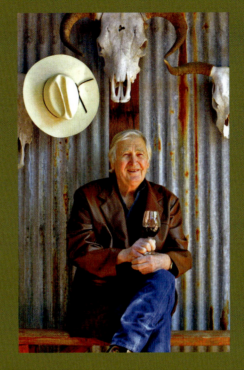

FESS PARKER

Texas native Fess Parker became one of the mid-century's most beloved television stars, known internationally for playing American icons Davy Crockett and Daniel Boone. He walked away from that lucrative career in the early 1970s to grow grapes and make fine wines under his name. As a result, he became just as big a star in the wine world as he had been in Hollywood. His family has continued the winemaking tradition along what is now known as the Foxen Canyon Wine Trail near Los Olivos, California. Fess passed away in 2010. We miss his charm, straight-talking style, and wisdom. Our friendship now spans three generations. You can order the families' wines online at fessparker.com.

Southern Sweet Potatoes with Brown Sugar Pecans

SERVES 6 TO 8

SWEET POTATOES

Vegetable oil spray

3 pounds sweet potatoes, preferably Garnet or another deeply colored variety

1 cup granulated sugar

6 tablespoons (¾ stick) salted butter

½ cup whole milk

3 large eggs, lightly beaten

1½ teaspoons pure vanilla extract

BROWN SUGAR-PECAN TOPPING

1 cup chopped pecans

1 cup packed brown sugar

Scant ½ cup all-purpose flour

¼ cup (½ stick) salted butter, melted

Regular Steakhouse guests start asking, about halfway through football season, when this fall favorite will be on the menu. We usually wait until just before Thanksgiving to roll it out. Credit goes to Lisa's mom for this holiday treat, sweet enough to serve for dessert. In addition to catering, we do a brisk business in big take-out trays of some of our staples, and these sweet potatoes are one of our most popular offerings.

1. To Prepare the Sweet Potatoes: Heat the oven to 350°F. Mist a 9 x 13-inch shallow baking dish with vegetable oil spray.

Use a fork to poke holes in each sweet potato. Put the sweet potatoes on a baking sheet and bake for 50 to 60 minutes, until very tender when pierced with a fork. Remove the sweet potatoes and leave the oven on.

When cool enough to handle, cut each sweet potato open lengthwise and scoop out the flesh—it should slide right out—into a bowl. Discard the peels. Mash the flesh well with a potato masher and add the granulated sugar, butter, milk, eggs, and vanilla. With a hand mixer on medium speed, beat to combine until the mixture is thin, light, and fluffy. Spoon the mixture into the prepared baking dish.

2. To Make the Topping: Stir the pecans, brown sugar, and flour together in a bowl. Stir in the melted butter until well combined. Spread the topping over the sweet potatoes.

3. Bake for 35 to 45 minutes, until the pecan topping is crunchy and the sweet potato mixture is hot and bubbly throughout. Serve hot.

Black-Eyed Peas with Bacon and Jalapeños

SERVES 6 TO 8

2 slices thick bacon

Three 15.5-ounce cans black-eyed peas, drained, liquid reserved from 1 can

1 or 2 pickled jalapeños, chopped

Kosher salt

A favorite Southern tradition, eating black-eyed peas on the first day of the new year, has long been associated with good luck. Once, when we were visiting Fess Parker and his family at their winery in California's Santa Ynez wine region over the New Year's holiday, we were flabbergasted to learn that our friends had no knowledge of this tradition. There were no black-eyed peas to be found within miles of their home. Ever since, when traveling over New Year's, we make sure we pack a few cans of black-eyed peas. While black-eyed peas go particularly well with fried catfish (page 184), you can serve them with just about anything.

1. Put the bacon slices in a cold skillet. Turn the heat to medium-low and cook the bacon for 3 minutes on one side. Turn the bacon and cook on the other side to desired doneness. Remove the bacon with a slotted spoon and drain on paper towels. Save the bacon drippings in the skillet. When cool enough to handle, crumble the bacon with your fingers and set aside.

2. Add the crumbled bacon, peas and reserved liquid, and jalapeños to the bacon drippings in the skillet. Taste and add salt, if you wish. Cook over medium heat for 5 minutes for the flavors to blend. Serve hot.

Ranch Pintos

SERVES 6 TO 8

1 pound dried pinto beans, sorted through for any stones or dirt, then rinsed

¼ pound salt pork or bacon, chopped

3 or 4 garlic cloves, minced

1 tablespoon chili powder

Kosher salt

Nothing's more essential to ranch and chuck wagon cooking than a hearty pot of pinto beans. This is because preserved salt pork as well as dried beans could be carried along the trail to easily make a hearty, stick-to-the-ribs filler that could be flavored up in different ways. You may not be out on a cattle drive, but if you have a pot of beans, you too have dinner. And perhaps in the time-honored way: a bowl of pintos with a wedge of corn-bread. Or strain and spoon the beans into a flour tortilla and build a burrito. Pinto beans are also a good side with any pork dish or Texas barbecue.

1. Put the beans in a large stockpot or Dutch oven and cover with cold water by at least 2 inches. Add the salt pork and garlic and bring to a boil over high heat. Reduce the heat to a simmer and cook the beans, uncovered, until they are creamy and tender, up to 2 hours. Check the beans several times during the cooking, stirring them up from the bottom. Add hot water as needed to keep the water level at least an inch above the beans.

2. Stir the chili powder and salt to taste into the beans and cook over low heat for another 15 minutes. There should be some liquid remaining in the pot.

3. Serve warm with two or more spoonfuls of the potlikker. The beans can be refrigerated and kept for several days; they are even better when reheated.

Jalapeño Cheese Grits

SERVES 6 OR MORE

¼ cup (½ stick) salted butter, plus more for the baking dish

1 large egg, well-beaten

2 tablespoons heavy cream (preferably), half-and-half, or whole milk

¾ cup (6 ounces) shredded mild Cheddar cheese

⅓ cup minced and seeded jalapeños

4 cups low-sodium chicken stock

1 cup quick-cooking grits, such as Quaker

Kosher salt

Nothing illustrates South by Southwest fare better than cheesy grits laced with jalapeño. With Lisa's Southern roots, it's the ultimate comfort food at our house served for breakfast, lunch, or dinner. While store-bought chicken stock is a great timesaver, try making your own (see sidebar) for the best flavor.

1. Heat the oven to 350°F. Butter a shallow 7x11-inch baking dish.

2. Combine the egg, cream, Cheddar, and jalapeños in a bowl and mix.

3. Combine the stock and butter in a large saucepan and bring to a boil over high heat. Over 2 to 3 minutes, sprinkle in the grits, about ¼ cup at a time, whisking continually to eliminate any lumps. Reduce the heat to a simmer. Switch from a whisk to a rubber spatula and continue to cook, stirring frequently, for 5 minutes, until the grits are thickened and coat the back of the spatula. Spoon out a teaspoon of the grits, let cool briefly, and taste for salt. Add more as necessary. Remove the saucepan from the heat and stir in the egg-jalapeño-cheese mixture. Pour the grits into the prepared baking dish.

4. Cover the dish with aluminum foil and bake for 30 minutes. Uncover and bake for an additional 10 minutes, until the grits are lightly puffed up and golden. Let rest for 5 to 10 minutes before serving.

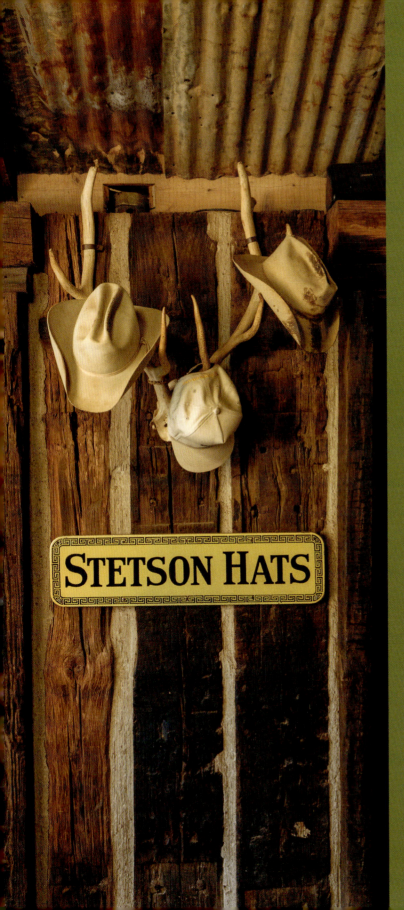

MAKING STOCK

For homemade chicken stock, use this as a guide. Add less onion or more carrot, for example, depending upon what you have on hand, and your wishes.

Warm 2 tablespoons olive oil in a large stockpot over medium-high heat. Working in two batches, add 3 pounds chicken parts (backs, wings, wing tips, thighs, and/or legs), skin side down. Brown well, then turn and brown the other side. Remove from the pot and brown the remaining chicken. Return the first batch to the pot and add 1 large yellow onion, quartered; 1 large carrot and 1 celery rib (including the leaves), both cut in 2-inch pieces; 1 bunch parsley; and a couple of bay leaves. Cover with about 5 quarts cold water. Bring to a boil over high heat, then reduce to a simmer. Cook uncovered for 3 to 4 hours, skimming off any scum and fat that rise to the top, until richly flavored. Place a colander over another large pot and carefully pour in the hot stock and solids. Press down on the solids to get out all of the goodness, then discard the solids. Bring the stock to a boil over high heat, then reduce the heat. Simmer until the stock is reduced to about 6 cups. Let cool, then refrigerate for up to a week, or freeze for up to several months.

Mac 'n' Cheese
with Roasted Poblanos

SERVES 6 OR MORE

Butter, for the baking dish

BREAD CRUMBS

1 tablespoon extra virgin olive oil

1 cup panko

CHEESE SAUCE

½ cup (1 stick) salted butter

2 tablespoons all-purpose flour

1 garlic clove, minced

1 cup whole milk

½ cup heavy cream

¾ teaspoon kosher salt

2 cups (8 ounces) shredded sharp Cheddar cheese

4 ounces fresh goat cheese, crumbled

¼ cup grated Parmesan cheese

¼ cup buttermilk, sour cream, or plain full-fat yogurt

MACARONI

2 teaspoons kosher salt

¾ pound elbow macaroni

2 poblano chiles, roasted, peeled, seeded, and chopped (page 219)

We were asked to cater a Texas wedding where the bride had her heart set on serving macaroni and cheese. We had never thought of serving mac 'n' cheese alongside our Mesquite Smoked Peppered Beef Tenderloin, but she was determined. If you're going to serve mac 'n' cheese, it has to be a really good one, and here it is! The dish was such a hit with the bride, groom, and their families and guests that we ended up serving it at the weddings of the bride's three sisters.

1. Heat the oven to 375°F. Butter a 9x13-inch baking dish.

2. To Toast the Bread Crumbs: Warm the oil in a small skillet over medium heat. Stir in the panko and toast until golden, stirring frequently. Turn off the heat and set aside.

3. To Make the Sauce: Melt the butter in a large saucepan over medium-low heat. Whisk the flour into the butter until incorporated, then cook for 2 to 3 minutes, stirring frequently. Stir in the garlic, raise the heat to medium-high, and gradually whisk in the milk and cream. Add the salt. Bring the mixture to a boil and continue to stir until thickened, about 4 minutes. Reduce the heat to medium-low and stir in the Cheddar, goat cheese, and Parmesan. Remove from the heat as soon as the cheeses have melted. Stir in the buttermilk. Cover to keep the sauce warm.

4. To Make the Macaroni: Bring a large pot of water to a boil. Stir in the salt and add the macaroni. Cook, stirring occasionally, for 6 to 8 minutes, just until the macaroni is al dente. Drain the macaroni in a colander; do not rinse. In a large bowl, combine the macaroni, cheese sauce, and poblanos. Spoon the mixture into the prepared baking dish.

5. Evenly scatter the toasted crumbs over the casserole. Bake for 30 minutes, until the mac 'n' cheese is heated through and the top is golden brown and crunchy. Let sit at room temperature for 5 minutes before serving.

BISCUITS & BREADS

A ranch cook's reputation has always been made or broken by the quality of the Dutch oven biscuits or sourdough bread. While today, most people have access to plenty of bakery versions of these, along with cornbread and other baked goods, it's extra-flavorful to make these for yourselves. What a sense of accomplishment too. Bread used to accompany every meal, a tradition we think is worth bringing back, especially when they're as flavorful as these.

Buttermilk Biscuits with Honey Butter

MAKES TWELVE 2½- TO 3-INCH BISCUITS

HONEY BUTTER

½ cup (1 stick) salted butter

2 tablespoons honey

BISCUITS

2 cups all-purpose flour, plus more for rolling out dough

2 teaspoons baking powder

½ teaspoon baking soda

¾ teaspoon table salt

¼ cup (½ stick) cold salted butter, cubed

1 cup buttermilk

Sourdough starter, a natural yeast mixture, was the leavening of choice for making biscuits and breads on the trail and is still used at the Steakhouse. Using buttermilk, baking powder, and baking soda in place of a starter imparts some of that tangy sourdough flavor to these light biscuits, which are easy to whip up. And oh my, are they good. The secret to great biscuits is to not overwork the dough. Brushing them with honey butter makes them irresistible.

1. Heat the oven to 450°F.

2. To Make the Honey Butter: Melt the butter in a small saucepan. Pour 1 tablespoon butter into a small dish and reserve it for brushing on the baked biscuits. Stir the honey into the remaining butter and let it melt.

3. To Make the Biscuits: Whisk together the flour, baking powder, baking soda, and salt in a large, shallow bowl. Add the cold butter cubes and use your fingers or a pastry blender to cut it into the flour mixture, making small pea-size pieces. Add the buttermilk. With a minimum of handling, mix into a smooth dough.

Put the dough on a lightly floured work surface. With a rolling pin, roll out to a generous ½-inch thickness. Using a floured 2½- to 3-inch biscuit cutter, cut the dough into rounds, as close together as possible to avoid having to reroll the dough. Between cutting out the biscuits, dip the cutter into some flour so the dough doesn't stick. Lightly pat together any remaining dough scraps, reroll gently, and cut into additional rounds.

4. Arrange the biscuits, barely touching, on a baking sheet. Bake until risen and golden brown, about 10 minutes. Lightly brush the tops with the reserved melted butter. Give the warm honey butter a good stir and pour into a small bowl to serve with the biscuits.

CHEDDAR–BLACK PEPPER BISCUITS: Add 1 teaspoon cracked black pepper to the flour mixture. Reduce the cubed butter to 3 tablespoons. Stir ¾ cup shredded Cheddar in with the wet ingredients. Continue as directed.

Sourdough Bread

Since Tom's a bona fide cowboy cook, we often make sourdough bread at the Steakhouse. Back before commercial yeast and baking powder, this natural yeast technique was essential for making bread and biscuits and flapjacks too. Like the chuck wagon cooks of old, Tom has kept a crock of sourdough starter alive for years. But he doesn't sleep with it the way the "cookies" on the range did to ensure that cold weather didn't kill off the yeast and bacteria that would leaven the breads. Today, we have a crock of sourdough starter in our fridge at home. It's fed once a month and we make a point to make bread once a month, just to keep the starter happy. It helps keep us happy too. Bread making's relatively easy, once you get going, and every time, we're amazed at the beauty of the bread.

It's a fairly lengthy process to get a sourdough starter—well—started. After that, you need to care for it as you would any living thing, keeping it fed, exercised, and made to feel useful by putting it to work regularly. When making any new dough or batter with sourdough, the starter is mixed with new flour and liquid, allowed to ferment and rise, and then some of that dough is mixed back into the starter crock. Many folks tried out the technique during the pandemic, when they had extra time on their hands. It's still worth slowing down and trying on occasion. We add a little commercial yeast to the mixture to make it foolproof and ready in about one day's time, rather than the three or more sometimes required.

Sourdough Starter

2 cups whole milk

One ¼-ounce package active dry yeast (about 2½ teaspoons)

½ cup lukewarm water

1½ cups all-purpose flour

1 cup granulated sugar

1 small russet potato, peeled and grated on the coarse holes of a box grater

1. Heat the milk over medium heat just until bubbles form around the edges of the pan. Meanwhile, combine the water and yeast in a crock or ceramic or glass bowl (metal would corrode) large enough to hold all of the starter's ingredients. Pour in the milk, then mix in the sugar and flour. Once incorporated, knead in the potato. Cover the mixture and let it stand at room temperature for 24 hours or more before using. It should have developed a mild, not unpleasant sour aroma. If a tan liquid forms on the top of the starter, mix it back in. This is just alcohol formed as a by-product of the fermentation process. Refrigerate the starter if not using within a day or two.

2. Either use or replenish the starter every couple of weeks. Use or discard at least 1 cup of it. Replace ½ cup each of flour and water for each cup used, mix in, and cover and let sit at room temperature for a day before refrigerating again.

Sourdough Bread

MAKES 1 LOAF

1 cup Sourdough Starter (page 243)

2½ cups lukewarm water (90°F)

5 cups all-purpose flour, or more as needed

1 tablespoon table salt

1. Place the starter in the work bowl of a heavy-duty stand mixer with a dough hook. Pour in the water and begin to mix slowly. The starter should dissolve partially, becoming soupy. Add the 5 cups of flour about 1 cup at a time, while continuing to mix. When all of the flour is incorporated, add the salt. Set the mixture aside, cover with a damp towel, and let it sit for 18 to 24 hours, until the dough is bubbly and risen to about twice its original size.

2. Return the work bowl to the mixer and, with medium speed, mix for about 5 minutes. The dough should go from wet, sticky, and stretchy to satiny. (You can get similar results by mixing the dough by hand, then kneading it for about 10 minutes.) Add a bit more flour if needed to get the proper texture. Cover the bowl with a damp cloth and let it rise in a warm, draft-free spot until doubled in size, 4 to 6 hours. Alternatively, refrigerate the dough for up to a day, then let it return to room temperature before proceeding.

3. Remove the dough from the bowl and, on a work surface, punch it down and divide it into 2 balls to make 2 free-form round loaves. (Alternatively, divide into 3 oblong pieces, and place in 3 oiled loaf pans.) Place the dough balls on a floured baking sheet, cover with large inverted bowls, and let them rise in a warm, draft-free spot until larger by half, 2 to 4 more hours.

4. Near the end of the rising time, heat the oven to 400°F. Bake for 40 to 45 minutes, until the bread is deeply brown on top and sounds hollow when thumped. Cool the loaves to room temperature on a baking rack. Eat within several hours for the best flavor, though the bread keeps at room temperature for several days and makes especially great toast (such as in the recipe on page 246).

Grilled Sourdough Slices with Green Onion Butter

SERVES 8 OR MORE

½ cup (1 stick) salted butter, at room temperature

¼ cup thinly sliced (⅛ inch) green onion tops

1 plump garlic clove, minced

One 1-pound sourdough loaf (page 244 for homemade), unsliced

Whether you whip up your own loaves of sourdough or buy them at a bakery, we think you'll find this one of the best ways to enjoy the bread. The flavor-packed butter can be made ahead, then you can grill some slices of the bread when you have other food over the fire.

1. In a bowl, mash together the butter, green onion tops, and garlic. Refrigerate the green onion butter until firm, about 1 hour. When you are ready to use the butter, let it sit at room temperature for 20 to 30 minutes.

2. You have a few grilling options: You can put the bread slices around the cooler edges of a hot fire; over the cooler side of a two-level fire; or over a medium-heat fire (4 to 5 seconds with the hand test—see page 147) used for grilling vegetables. If grilling over gas or charcoal, add several mesquite chunks to the fire shortly before placing the bread on the grill.

3. Cut the sourdough bread into 1-inch-thick slices. Toast the bread on the grill on each side for 1 to 2 minutes, until lightly browned, with grill marks. Immediately slather one side of each slice with the onion butter. Serve right away as the butter is melting into the slices, so each bite is soft as well as crunchy.

BREAD CRUMBS

We always have plenty of leftover sourdough bread around the restaurant kitchen. Rather than toss it, we make our own version of large, flaky panko-style bread crumbs. Take four or so large, thick slices of day-old bread and brush them generously with extra virgin olive oil. Put them on a baking sheet and bake at 350°F for about 20 minutes, turning the bread once halfway through. The bread is ready when deeply golden brown. Once the bread cools, use the large-hole side of a cheese grater to make coarse crumbs.

Skillet Cornbread

Vegetable oil spray

2 cups buttermilk

2 large eggs

2 to 3 drops pure vanilla extract

2 cups stone-ground yellow cornmeal

2 tablespoons granulated sugar, optional

1½ teaspoons table salt

1 teaspoon baking soda

¼ cup (½ stick) salted butter, melted

There's something so darned familiar and satisfying about a cast-iron skillet of cornbread, kind of like slipping into your favorite old flannel shirt. Serve it with chili or any barbecue. Our favorite summer dinner is a bowl of black-eyed peas and a plate of sliced tomatoes from the garden and some skillet cornbread. If you think that sugar only belongs in iced tea, by all means omit it.

1. Heat the oven to 450°F. Mist an 8-inch cast-iron skillet with vegetable oil spray. Put the skillet in the oven to heat while preparing the cornbread.

2. Whisk together the buttermilk, eggs, and vanilla in a mixing bowl. In a separate bowl, combine the cornmeal, sugar (if using), salt, and baking soda.

3. Add the buttermilk mixture and melted butter to the dry ingredients and stir just until combined. Pour the batter into the hot skillet.

4. Bake for 15 to 18 minutes, until just firm and golden brown on top. Let the bread cool for 5 minutes before slicing into wedges.

Cheddar-Jalapeño Cornbread

SERVES 8

Vegetable oil spray

4 jalapeños

2 cups stone-ground yellow cornmeal

½ cup all-purpose flour

3 tablespoons granulated sugar

4 teaspoons table salt

1 teaspoon baking soda

¼ teaspoon baking powder

2 cups whole milk

2 large eggs

8 ounces (2 cups) shredded Cheddar cheese

2 tablespoons salted butter, melted

Here's a moister, spicier cornbread. It's not as hot as you might guess from the quantity of jalapeños because the cheese and milk douse some of the heat. Jalapeños are so ubiquitous in Texas food today that it may be surprising to realize that they weren't commonly associated with Tex-Mex or other local dishes until the 1960s, about the time that Texan Lyndon B. Johnson succeeded John F. Kennedy as president in 1963. All things Texas enjoyed a burst of recognition, from barbecued brisket to the hot little chile, originally from the Mexican state of Veracruz, known as the jalapeño.

1. Heat the oven to 325°F. Mist a shallow 9x13-inch baking dish with vegetable oil spray.

2. Spear the jalapeños on a large fork and hold them over the flame of a gas stove burner. Turn until all sides are blackened and blistered. Immediately put the peppers into a plastic bag, seal, and let them steam and cool for 5 minutes. (If you don't have a gas stove, grill or broil the jalapeños as directed on page 219.)

3. While the jalapeños cool, whisk together the cornmeal, flour, sugar, salt, baking soda, and baking powder in a large bowl.

4. Pull any skin that is loose off the jalapeños, but otherwise leave the blackened skin in place to add a little deeper flavor to the cornbread. Seed and mince the jalapeños. Whisk together the jalapeños, milk, and eggs in a bowl. Stir the wet ingredients into the dry, just until combined. Don't overmix. Gently stir in the Cheddar. Pour into the prepared baking dish.

5. Bake for 40 to 45 minutes, until golden on top and a toothpick inserted into the center comes out clean. Set the dish on a wire baking rack and brush the top of the cornbread with the melted butter. Let sit for 5 minutes. Slice and serve warm or at room temperature.

Gingerbread

MAKES 4 OR 5 MINI LOAVES

Vegetable oil spray

2 cups all-purpose flour

1 pound dark brown sugar
(2¼ packed cups)

¾ cup (1½ sticks) salted butter,
at room temperature

1 teaspoon baking soda

2 teaspoons ground cinnamon

1 teaspoon ground nutmeg

½ teaspoon ground ginger

1 cup buttermilk

2 large eggs

TOM'S TIP: These small loaves make the best gifts and party favors too. If you prefer, though, to make one large loaf in a 9 x 5-inch pan, add about 10 minutes to the baking time.

This was the first bread we gifted to visitors who stayed overnight in our Perini Ranch Guest Quarters. We still offer this loaf in winter, but rotate with other breads such as the Banana-Nut Bread that follows on page 252. It's not the easiest of recipes, but the results are worth it. Sometimes, we'll have a loaf that falls in the oven, and the good news is, that's the one for the folks working in the kitchen, and we think the best!

1. Heat the oven to 375°F. Mist five mini loaf pans (approximately 3½ x 5½ inches) with vegetable oil spray. We've found pan sizes to be a bit inconsistent. If yours are slightly larger than specified, you may just get four loaves.

2. Whisk together the flour and brown sugar in a large bowl. Using your fingers, work in the butter until the mixture is crumbly. Scoop out 1 cup of the mixture and set aside to use as a topping.

3. To the flour mixture in the bowl, add the baking soda, cinnamon, nutmeg, and ginger.

4. Whisk together the buttermilk and eggs in a small bowl. Using the whisk, mix the wet ingredients into the dry until well combined. Divide the batter among the prepared pans.

5. Bake for 10 minutes, then quickly sprinkle the loaves with the reserved topping. Return the pans to the oven and continue baking for 8 to 10 minutes longer, until a toothpick inserted into the centers comes out clean.

6. Run a dinner knife around the inside of each pan and pop out each loaf. Place them top up on a wire baking rack to cool. Slice and serve. Wrap extra loaves in zippered freezer bags and keep at room temperature for a couple of days, or in the freezer for up to a month.

MAKES 2 LOAVES

Butter, for the baking dish

TOPPING

½ cup packed light brown sugar

½ cup all-purpose flour

1 teaspoon ground cinnamon

¼ cup (½ stick) unsalted butter, at room temperature

⅓ cup chopped pecans, lightly toasted in a dry skillet

DRY INGREDIENTS

1½ cups all-purpose flour

1 teaspoon baking soda

1 teaspoon ground cinnamon

¾ teaspoon table salt

½ cup chopped pecans, lightly toasted in a dry skillet

WET INGREDIENTS

3 very ripe bananas, peeled and mashed

2 large eggs, lightly beaten

½ cup sour cream

1 teaspoon pure vanilla extract

CREAMED INGREDIENTS

½ cup unsalted butter, at room temperature

¼ cup granulated sugar

½ cup packed light brown sugar

Banana-Nut Bread

We offer small loaves of this bread in our Guest Quarters as a breakfast option, as well as rotate it through The Gap Café menu. Don't hesitate to enjoy a slice though, any time of day, with a cup of tea or even a shot of bourbon. It's nicely moist from the banana puree, sour cream, and butter, so it keeps well for several days and freezes well too. The contrasting crunchy streusel topping really makes it. You'll use a few bowls, but we promise, it's well worth it.

1. Heat the oven to 325°F. Butter 2 loaf pans that are approximately 9x5 inches. Dust with flour, shaking out any excess.

2. To Make the Topping: In a small bowl, stir together the brown sugar, flour, cinnamon, and butter. When well combined and crumbly, mix in the pecans. Set aside.

3. In a medium bowl, stir together the dry ingredients. In another medium bowl, combine the wet ingredients. In the bowl of an electric mixer, beat the creamed ingredients together over medium-high speed, about 2 minutes, until light and fluffy. Stop the mixer and pour in the wet ingredients. Beat over medium speed to combine, about 1 minute more. Scrape down the sides of the bowl as needed to mix evenly. Add the dry ingredients about half at a time, continuing to beat over medium speed, until just combined.

4. Scrape the batter into the prepared pans and smooth the top with a rubber spatula. Scatter half of the topping over each loaf. Bake about 45 minutes, or until a toothpick inserted in the center comes out clean. Cool loaves in pans on a baking rack for 10 to 15 minutes. Run a knife around the edges of each loaf and remove them from the pans. Let cool completely before slicing.

DESSERTS

In a nation known for its sweet tooth, Texans still take the cake. So we have cakes, like the perennially popular chocolate sheet cake, and the more contemporary fave, tres leches. But we have so much more for a sweet finish, from the bread pudding that Tom crafted for a cowboy symposium to the strawberry shortcake his great-grandmother created. We make cobblers, and crisps, and cheesecakes, and those other Southern staples, banana pudding and pecan pie, and much more. Join us at the dessert table. It will be worth it!

Sourdough Bread Pudding with Bourbon Sauce

SERVES 8 TO 10

BREAD PUDDING

Vegetable oil spray

2 large eggs

2½ cups whole milk

2 tablespoons salted butter, melted

2 tablespoons pure vanilla extract

1½ cups granulated sugar

4 packed cups 1-inch-cubed sourdough bread (day-old bread is fine)

⅓ cup chopped pecans

BOURBON SAUCE

½ cup (1 stick) salted butter

½ cup heavy whipping cream

½ cup granulated sugar

¼ cup bourbon

Back in the 1980s, Tom was planning to attend the Chuckwagon Cook-Off at New Mexico's Lincoln County Cowboy Symposium—a major event in ranching culture. The cook-off was offering an unheard-of $3,000 prize for the best dish. Tom knew it would take something different than the usual chuck wagon fare to snag first place. He developed this bread pudding using sourdough bread in a Dutch oven. He added Texas pecans and topped the pudding with a rich, bourbon-laced sauce. Tom won the day and the prize money. This dessert has been on our menu every day since and is our bestseller.

1. Heat the oven to 325°F. Mist a 9- or 10-inch square baking dish with vegetable oil spray.

2. To Make the Bread Pudding: Whisk the eggs until lightly beaten, then add the milk, melted butter, and vanilla. Gradually add the sugar and continue to whisk until the sugar has dissolved.

Arrange the bread cubes in the baking dish. Pour the egg-milk mixture over the bread. Press down on the bread lightly, just enough to make sure all the bread cubes are saturated. Sprinkle the pecans over the bread, lightly pushing them down into the bread as well.

Bake the bread pudding for about 50 minutes, until golden and crusty, but still moist below the top crust.

3. To Make the Sauce: While the pudding bakes, combine the butter, cream, sugar, and bourbon in a saucepan. Bring to a boil, stirring occasionally, and then remove from the heat.

4. Serve the warm pudding in bowls, topped with a healthy drizzle of the warm sauce.

Texas Chocolate Sheet Cake

SERVES 16 OR MORE

CAKE

Vegetable oil spray

1 cup (2 sticks) salted butter

¼ cup unsweetened cocoa

2 cups all-purpose flour

2 cups granulated sugar

2 large eggs, beaten lightly

½ cup buttermilk

1 teaspoon pure vanilla extract

1 teaspoon baking soda

½ teaspoon ground cinnamon

FROSTING

½ cup (1 stick) salted butter

¼ cup unsweetened cocoa

¼ cup plus 2 tablespoons whole milk

1 pound (3½ cups) confectioners' sugar, plus additional for serving

1 teaspoon pure vanilla extract

1 cup chopped pecans

Just about every heritage cookbook published by a Junior League, a family, or a historical society in Texas includes a version of this fudgy treat. Much of its appeal to Texans is its sheer size, since it's baked on a large baking sheet rather than in round cake pans. Both the cake and the frosting should be warm when you put them together. The cake easily cuts into squares, making it a great choice for any celebration.

This particular version was popularized in the 1960s by Texan Lady Bird Johnson, First Lady of the United States, when Lyndon Baines Johnson was president.

1. **To Make the Cake:** Heat the oven to 350°F. Mist a 13 x 18-inch rimmed baking sheet with vegetable oil spray.

Melt the butter in a large saucepan over medium heat. Remove the pan from the heat and add 1 cup water and the cocoa, stirring well. Whisk together the flour and granulated sugar in a bowl, then whisk into the chocolate mixture. Whisk together the eggs, buttermilk, vanilla, baking soda, and cinnamon in a mixing bowl. Pour the chocolate-flour mixture into the egg-buttermilk mixture and whisk again until well combined.

Pour the cake batter onto the baking sheet, spreading it evenly. Bake for 18 to 20 minutes, rotating the baking sheet from back to front once after about 10 minutes. When the cake is done, a toothpick inserted into the center will come out clean.

2. **To Make the Frosting:** While the cake is baking, melt the butter with the cocoa in a large saucepan over medium heat. Add the milk and bring just to a boil. Whisk in the confectioners' sugar, stirring well to eliminate any clumps. Remove the frosting from the heat and use a spatula to fold in the vanilla and pecans. Immediately pour the thin frosting over the warm cake, spreading it quickly and evenly.

3. Cool completely, then slice to serve.

TEXAS ROYALTY

It has been our honor to cater for the Bush family at the Texas Governor's Mansion, the White House, and their ranch in Crawford. While President George W. Bush has long been a big fan of The President's Pecan Pie (page 264), he became even more excited about our Texas Chocolate Sheet Cake. When Laura Bush spoke with Lisa about catering the Bushes' joint 70th birthday celebration at their Central Texas ranch, she said that George W. insisted on having the cake. To serve the many guests who would be attending, Lisa came up with the idea of stacking four sheet cakes on top of one another.

Following the meal, we were asked to carry out the cake personally while Texas country music legend George Strait serenaded the guests and then broke out into "Happy Birthday." It was all quite festive, but never did we dream that escorting the cake would land us on the pages of *People* magazine.

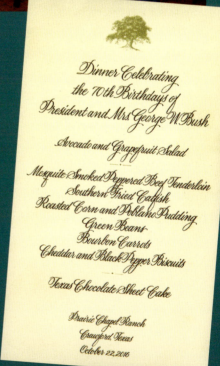

Dinner Celebrating
the 70th Birthdays of
President and Mrs George W Bush

Avocado and Grapefruit Salad

Mesquite Smoked Peppered Beef Tenderloin
Southern Fried Catfish
Roasted Corn and Poblano Pudding
Green Beans
Bourbon Carrots
Cheddar and Black Pepper Biscuits

Texas Chocolate Sheet Cake

Prairie Chapel Ranch
Crawford, Texas
October 22, 2016

Tres Leches Cake

One 18.25-ounce plain yellow cake mix, preferably Duncan Hines, prepared according to package directions and baked in a 9x13-inch cake pan

One 14-ounce can sweetened condensed milk

One 12-ounce can evaporated milk

¾ cup whole milk

Vegetable oil spray

2 cups heavy whipping cream

2 tablespoons confectioners' sugar

Raspberries or other berries, optional

A relatively recent import from Mexico and Latin America, tres leches refers to three milks—sweetened condensed, evaporated, and whole—that are combined and allowed to soak into a baked yellow cake, making it soft and super silky. We added it to our repertoire when we hosted a party in honor of Tom's daughter Jessica, with the theme of "A Night in Old Mexico," inspired by a trip to San Miguel de Allende. A July night can be hot enough to melt butter on the sidewalk, so we wanted something that would be refreshing. We used a cake mix for ease and simplicity. The whipped cream topping cuts some of the sweetness of this crowd-pleasing, luscious dessert. Berries on the side are welcome, but not a necessity.

1. While the cake is still warm, gently prick it all over with a fork about every ½ inch. Put the condensed, evaporated, and whole milks in a bowl and mix. Slowly pour the milk mixture over the cake, saturating it evenly and thoroughly. Let the cake sit at room temperature for 30 minutes to cool. Cover the cake with plastic wrap sprayed with vegetable oil spray. Refrigerate for 30 to 60 minutes.

2. While the cake is chilling, combine the cream and confectioners' sugar in the bowl of a stand mixer with the whisk attachment. Beat on high speed until stiff peaks form. Uncover the cake and spread the whipped cream on top. Cover the cake again and return to the refrigerator for at least 1 hour, or up to 12 hours. Slice and serve with berries, if desired.

Banana Pudding

SERVES 6

½ cup granulated sugar

1 tablespoon cornstarch

¼ teaspoon kosher salt

3 large egg yolks

¾ cup whole milk

½ cup half-and-half

1½ teaspoons pure vanilla extract

4 ounces (1 cup) Cool Whip whipped topping, thawed

18 vanilla wafer cookies, plus 6 cookies for serving

2 medium bananas

This childhood favorite delights diners of all ages. We serve it in half-pint Mason jars with the metal ring screwed on for a touch of nostalgia. If you're planning to take the pudding jars to a picnic or other event, put on the lids as well.

Slice the bananas just before serving so they don't turn brown. For big parties, we nestle the jars in a big, galvanized metal tub of ice so everyone can help themselves.

We use Cool Whip, because it holds its height much better than whipped cream.

1. Stir together the sugar, cornstarch, and salt in a heavy saucepan. Whisk in the egg yolks, followed by the milk and half-and-half. Cook the pudding over medium-low heat, stirring frequently, until thick enough to coat the back of a spoon. It will take 15 to 20 minutes for the pudding to thicken. Remove the pudding from the heat and stir in the vanilla.

2. Using a spatula, fold in the Cool Whip by hand until there are no streaks. Refrigerate the pudding for up to an hour. To store the pudding for up to a day, place a piece of plastic wrap directly on the pudding's surface to prevent a skin from forming.

3. Put the 18 cookies in a zippered plastic bag and finely crush with a rolling pin. Set aside ½ cup cookie crumbs. Sprinkle equal portions of the remaining crumbs in the bottoms of 6 glasses. Spoon about ½ cup chilled pudding into each jar. Stand 1 whole cookie in the center of each pudding.

4. Peel and slice the bananas. Top each pudding serving with some banana slices, then sprinkle on the remaining cookie crumbs. Serve immediately.

Pear-Cranberry Crisp

SERVES 8

Butter, for the baking dish

TOPPING

½ cup all-purpose flour

½ cup packed brown sugar

¼ cup chopped pecans

½ teaspoon ground cinnamon

¼ cup (½ stick) salted butter, cubed, at room temperature

4 large ripe pears, preferably Anjou or Bartlett

4 ounces fresh or thawed frozen cranberries

4 teaspoons granulated sugar

Designed to serve eight people, this winter dessert has a nice festive feel to it. We cut four pears in half, pack cranberries into the cavities, and scatter a nutty crisp topping over each half.

1. Heat the oven to 375°F. Butter a 9-inch square baking dish.

2. **To Make the Topping:** Combine the flour, brown sugar, pecans, and cinnamon in a food processor. Give the processor a couple of pulses to combine a bit. Add the butter and pulse until the mixture is an evenly crumbly meal.

3. Peel the pears, then slice each lengthwise in half and core. If the pear halves are roly-poly, slice a very thin bit off each rounded side so they sit still in the baking dish. Place the pears in the dish, cut side up.

4. Mound one-eighth of the cranberries in the hollow of each pear half and sprinkle each with ½ teaspoon granulated sugar.

5. Spoon the topping over the pears evenly, mounding it over each pear and packing it down lightly. Scatter any remaining cranberries and topping around the pears. Bake the crisp for 40 to 45 minutes, until the topping is crunchy and the pears and cranberries are tender. Serve warm.

Lemon Semifreddo

SERVES 8

1 cup (about 12 large) egg yolks

¾ cup fresh lemon juice (from approximately 4 large lemons)

Zest from 2 lemons, minced

1¼ cups granulated sugar

¼ teaspoon table salt

½ teaspoon pure vanilla extract

2 cups heavy whipping cream

Approximately 4 cups mixed berries

Thin lemon slices, optional

Sort of like ice cream, sort of like mousse, semifreddo's a wonderful Italian frozen dessert combining lemon curd and whipped cream. It's refreshing and unexpected following a hearty meal. Raspberries or strawberries, or a mix of them with blueberries, can accompany the semifreddo. A few lemon slices look nice topping it off too. You'll want to start this one at least a few hours ahead of when you plan to serve it, though you can easily make it a day or two ahead, if you prefer.

1. Line a large loaf pan with a large piece of plastic wrap. You want to have overhang on all sides so that you can fold the plastic up over the semifreddo.

2. In a heavy medium saucepan, whisk together the egg yolks, lemon juice, lemon zest, sugar, and salt. Cook over low heat, whisking often, until the mixture thickens enough to coat the back of a spoon. It should get somewhat lighter and fluffier during the 10 or so minutes it should take you to get the proper consistency. Stir in the vanilla extract and remove from the heat. Spoon the lemon curd mixture through a strainer into a bowl and let it cool.

3. Whip the cream with an electric mixer until it forms soft peaks. Fold the lemon curd mixture into the whipped cream, about one-third at a time, until lightly mixed together.

4. Spoon the mixture into the loaf pan and smooth it down with a rubber spatula to eliminate air bubbles. Cover the mixture with the overhanging plastic and freeze for a minimum of 4 hours.

5. When ready to serve, use the plastic edges to pull the semifreddo from the pan. Cut into slices and serve immediately with berries, and if you wish, lemon slices.

The President's Pecan Pie

SERVES 8 TO 10

SINGLE-CRUST BUTTER-AND-LARD PIE DOUGH

1¼ cups all-purpose flour, plus more for rolling out

½ teaspoon table salt

3 tablespoons salted butter, cut into cubes and chilled

5 tablespoons lard, cut into cubes and chilled

2 to 4 tablespoons ice water

Vegetable oil spray

PECAN FILLING

4 large eggs, lightly beaten

1 cup light corn syrup

⅔ cup granulated sugar

3 tablespoons salted butter, melted

1 tablespoon pure vanilla extract

1½ generous cups coarsely chopped pecans

The most important pecan dish in Lone Star culture and cuisine is pecan pie. Our ranch, like much of Texas, is dotted with pecan trees, and we use pecans in everything from salads to spiced nuts. Lisa tested ten different pie recipes to find the one that appealed to us the most. It's intentionally not a trendy version with some load of chocolate or pumpkin or salted caramel. It's just a classic pie, and not tooth-achingly sweet. We have been very fortunate to cater for the Bush family at the Texas Governor's Mansion in Austin, and later while George W. Bush and First Lady Laura were in the White House and at their Texas homes. President Bush is very fond of this version of every Texan's favorite pie.

1. To Make the Pie Dough: Combine the flour and salt in a food processor and pulse briefly. Scatter the butter over the flour and pulse three or four times just to combine. Scatter the lard over the flour-butter mixture. Pulse several more times until the fats disappear into the flour. Sprinkle in 2 tablespoons ice water and pulse several times, just until the water is absorbed and the dough comes together.

Dump the dough onto a floured surface. Lightly rub the dough with your fingers, adding more water, 1 tablespoon at a time, as needed just to hold it together. Once the dough holds together, stop. Don't overwork the dough. Gently pat the dough into a 6-inch disk. Wrap in plastic wrap and refrigerate for at least 30 minutes or overnight.

Mist a 9-inch pie pan with vegetable oil spray. Roll out the dough on a floured surface into a thin 12-inch round. Fit the round into the prepared pie pan, avoiding stretching it. Crimp the edges, then refrigerate the crust for at least 15 minutes.

2. Heat the oven to 375°F.

3. To Make the Filling: Whisk together the eggs, corn syrup, sugar, butter, and vanilla in a bowl. Using a spatula, fold in the pecans. Pour the filling into the pie crust.

4. Bake the pie for 10 minutes, then reduce the temperature to 350°F. Bake for 35 to 40 minutes longer, until a toothpick inserted into the center comes out clean. Let the pie cool on a wire baking rack for at least 1 hour before slicing and serving.

Pecan Bars

MAKES 16

Vegetable oil spray

CRUST

2 cups all-purpose flour

½ cup granulated sugar

¼ teaspoon table salt

¾ cup (1½ sticks) salted butter, cubed and at room temperature

PECAN FILLING

3 large eggs

¾ cup packed light brown sugar

¾ cup light corn syrup

6 tablespoons (¾ stick) salted butter

1 teaspoon pure vanilla extract

2 cups finely chopped pecans

Packed with even more pecans than the pie on page 264, these bar cookies work when finger food makes a better finish to a meal than a plated piece of gooey pie requiring a fork. We often serve these side-by-side with the several bar cookies that follow.

1. To Make the Crust: Heat the oven to 300°F. Mist a 9-inch square baking dish with vegetable oil spray. Layer parchment paper in the pan so that 2 sides of it overhang, so that you will be able to pull the baked bars easily from the pan.

Combine the flour, granulated sugar, and salt in a food processor and pulse three or four times. Sprinkle the butter cubes on top of the flour mixture. Pulse until the dough is crumbly and holds together when pinched with your fingers. Put the dough into the prepared baking dish and use your fingers to press it into an even layer.

Bake for 15 to 20 minutes, until the crust is set and lightly browned. Leave the oven on.

2. To Make the Filling: Beat the eggs in the bowl of a stand mixer. In a saucepan, combine the brown sugar, corn syrup, and butter and bring to a boil over medium-high heat.

Remove from the heat and stir in the vanilla. Pour one-quarter of the brown sugar mixture into the eggs and beat for 15 seconds, just to combine. With the mixer running on medium, drizzle in the rest of the brown sugar mixture. Stop the mixer. Using a spatula, fold in the pecans.

3. Pour the filling over the crust. Bake for 25 to 30 minutes, until the filling is set. Let cool slightly. While still warm, run a table knife around the inside of the pan to loosen the bars, then let cool completely. Cut into squares.

Opposite: Pecan Bars, left, with Lemon-Rosemary Bars.

Lemon-Rosemary Bars

MAKES 16

Vegetable oil spray

CRUST

2 cups all-purpose flour

½ cup sifted confectioners' sugar

2 tablespoons finely chopped fresh rosemary leaves

¼ teaspoon table salt

¾ cup (1½ sticks) salted butter, cubed and at room temperature

LEMON FILLING

¼ cup plus 2 tablespoons all-purpose flour

1½ cups granulated sugar

¾ teaspoon baking powder

3 large eggs

2 tablespoons grated lemon zest

½ cup fresh lemon juice

1 tablespoon confectioners' sugar, for sprinkling

These bar cookies are a slightly more sophisticated take on the bake sale classic, lemon squares. The hint of rosemary adds an interesting twist.

1. To Make the Crust: Heat the oven to 350°F. Mist a 9-inch square pan with vegetable oil spray. Layer parchment paper in the pan so that 2 sides of it overhang, so that you will be able to pull the baked bars easily from the pan.

Combine the flour, confectioners' sugar, rosemary, and salt in a food processor and pulse three or four times. Sprinkle the butter cubes on top of the flour mixture. Pulse until the dough is crumbly and holds together when pinched with your fingers. Put the dough into the prepared baking sheet and use your fingers to press it into an even layer.

Bake for 16 to 18 minutes, until the crust is just set and barely colored. Leave the oven on, but reduce the heat to 325°F.

2. To Make the Filling: Whisk together the flour, granulated sugar, and baking powder in a large bowl. Whisk the eggs in a medium bowl. Add the lemon zest and juice to the eggs and whisk until well combined. Slowly stir the egg mixture into the flour mixture. Evenly pour the filling over the crust.

3. Bake for 20 to 25 minutes, until the filling is lightly set. Let cool slightly. While still warm, run a table knife around the inside of the pan to loosen the bars, then let cool completely. Cut into squares. Sprinkle with confectioners' sugar just before serving.

Apple Pie Bars

MAKES 16

Vegetable oil spray

CRUST

1 cup (2 sticks) unsalted butter, at room temperature

½ cup granulated sugar

¼ cup packed light brown sugar

2 teaspoons pure vanilla extract

2 cups all-purpose flour

¾ teaspoon kosher salt

TOPPING

¾ cup all-purpose flour

¾ cup packed light brown sugar

1½ teaspoons ground cinnamon

¼ cup (½ stick) unsalted butter, melted

FILLING

2 tablespoons granulated sugar

½ teaspoon ground cinnamon

Pinch of ground nutmeg

1 tablespoon fresh lemon juice

2 pounds tangy apples, such as Granny Smith, peeled, cored, and diced into bite-size pieces

½ cup (1 stick) unsalted butter

We came up with this to make a handheld version of an apple pie or crisp. The crust, easier to whip up than a pie crust, is pressed in, rather than rolled. It's sturdy, like shortbread, so it can hold the apple filling and streusel-like topping.

1. Heat the oven to 350°F. Mist a 9x13-inch baking pan with vegetable oil spray. Layer parchment paper in the pan so that 2 sides of it overhang so that you will be able to pull the baked bars easily from the pan.

2. To Make the Crust: Combine the butter and both sugars in the bowl of an electric mixer fitted with the paddle attachment. Beat over medium-high speed until light and creamy, about 2 minutes. Stir the flour and salt together and add them to the bowl, about one-third of the mixture at a time, beating to just combine between each addition. Press the dough evenly into the prepared dish. Refrigerate the crust for 20 minutes. Then bake for 18 to 20 minutes, until set and golden brown.

3. To Make the Topping: While the crust is baking, stir together the flour, butter, and cinnamon in a small bowl. Mix in the melted butter and set the topping aside.

4. To Make the Filling: Also while the crust is baking, combine the sugar, cinnamon, and nutmeg in a small bowl, then add the lemon juice. Stir in the apple slices, coating them evenly. Melt the butter in a medium skillet over medium heat. Add the apple slices and cook for 10 to 12 minutes, stirring frequently, until the liquid has mostly evaporated and the apples have reduced in size by about one-third. Spoon the apple mixture over the crust and smooth it almost to the edges. Sprinkle the topping over the apples. Bake 25 to 30 minutes, until the topping has crisped up and darkened a shade or two.

5. Let the bars cool thoroughly, at least several hours. Slice into bars. We usually make them about 1 x 2 inches, but you can cut them smaller or larger, if you wish.

Seven-Layer Bars

MAKES 16

Vegetable oil spray

2 cups graham cracker crumbs

½ cup (1 stick) plus 2 tablespoons unsalted butter, melted

¼ cup plus 2 tablespoons confectioners' sugar

2 cups semisweet chocolate chips

1 cup butterscotch chips

¾ cup white chocolate chips

½ cup chopped walnuts

One 14-ounce can sweetened condensed milk

1 cup sweetened shredded coconut

Here's a good one to make a day or even two ahead, and they're easy as pie. Well, actually, they're a lot easier than pie! Seven-layer bars are quite the American bake sale favorite, sometimes called magic bars or Hello Dolly bars. Don't argue over what to call them too long though, or they're likely to disappear before you get your fill. Recipes for these vary, but we favor a combo of graham cracker crust with semisweet chocolate, butterscotch, and white chocolate chips, along with crunchy walnuts and a layer of coconut that gets nicely toasted while baking.

1. Heat the oven to 350°F. Mist a 9x13-inch baking pan with vegetable oil spray. Layer parchment paper in the pan so that 2 sides of it overhang, so that you will be able to pull the baked bars easily from the pan.

2. In a medium bowl, mix together the graham crackers crumbs, butter, and confectioners' sugar. Press the mixture firmly into the baking pan. We use the bottom of a metal measuring cup to pack it into place. Scatter the chocolate, butterscotch chips, white chocolate chips, and walnuts evenly over the crust. Warm the sweetened condensed milk (to make it easier to pour, easily done in a microwave if you have one). Pour about three-quarters of the milk over the mixture, then sprinkle evenly with the coconut. Drizzle the remaining milk over the coconut. Bake for 25 to 30 minutes, until just set with lightly toasted coconut.

3. Let the bars mixture cool thoroughly, at least several hours. Slice into bars. We usually make them about 1x2 inches, but you can cut them smaller or larger, if you wish. They are quite rich.

Peach-Bourbon Cobbler

DOUBLE-CRUST BUTTER-AND-LARD PIE DOUGH

2½ cups all-purpose flour, plus more for rolling

1 teaspoon table salt

½ cup (1 stick) salted butter, cut into cubes and chilled

½ cup lard, cut into cubes and chilled

6 to 8 tablespoons ice water

Vegetable oil spray

PEACH FILLING

¾ cup (1½ sticks) salted butter

2 to 2½ pounds fresh or frozen peaches, peeled, pitted, and thinly sliced

1 cup heavy whipping cream

¾ cup packed brown sugar

½ cup granulated sugar, plus additional for sprinkling over the top

¾ teaspoon ground cinnamon, plus additional for sprinkling over the top

⅓ cup bourbon

Peaches from Central Texas are one of early summer's fleeting treats, and cobbler is the way we most often present them. A splash of bourbon makes a fine addition to the juicy filling. If you don't have access to fresh peaches, frozen ones are the next best choice. Top the warm cobbler with a scoop of vanilla ice cream, if desired.

1. To Make the Pie Dough: Combine the flour and salt in a food processor and pulse briefly. Scatter the butter over the flour and pulse three or four times just to combine. Scatter the lard over the flour-butter mixture. Pulse several more times until the fats disappear into the flour. Sprinkle in 6 tablespoons ice water and pulse several times, just until the water is absorbed and the dough comes together.

Dump the dough onto a floured surface. Lightly rub the dough with your fingers, adding more water, 1 tablespoon at a time, as needed just to hold it together. Once the dough holds together, stop. Don't overwork the dough. Divide the dough into two equal pieces. Gently pat each piece into a 6-inch disk. Wrap in plastic wrap and refrigerate for at least 30 minutes or overnight.

Heat the oven to 400°F. Mist a 9 x 13-inch baking dish with vegetable oil spray.

On a lightly floured surface, roll each dough piece into a 9 x 13-inch rectangle. Fit one rectangle in the bottom of the dish. Bake for 18 to 20 minutes, until lightly set. Remove the pan from the oven. Leave the oven on, but reduce the temperature to 350°F.

2. To Make the Filling: While the bottom crust is baking, melt the butter in a large saucepan. Stir in the peaches, cream, brown sugar, granulated sugar, and cinnamon and bring to a boil over high heat. Reduce the heat to low and simmer for 15 minutes, or until the peaches are tender. Stir in the bourbon and cook for another couple of minutes. Evenly pour the filling

over the bottom crust. Top with the second dough rectangle, tucking the edges in. Using a knife, cut four to six 1- to 2-inch slits in the top dough so steam can escape. Sprinkle the top lightly with sugar and cinnamon.

3. Bake the cobbler for 40 to 45 minutes, until the top crust is crisp and golden. Let the cobbler sit for 15 minutes before serving.

Tom's Great-Grandmother's Strawberry Shortcake

SERVES 8

SUGAR BISCUITS

2 cups all-purpose flour, plus more for rolling out

⅓ cup granulated sugar, plus more for sprinkling

2 teaspoons baking powder

½ teaspoon baking soda

¾ teaspoon table salt

¼ cup (½ stick) salted butter

1 cup buttermilk

1 tablespoon salted butter, melted, for brushing

STRAWBERRIES

2 pounds fresh strawberries, green tops removed, halved vertically, and any white centers removed

½ cup granulated sugar

1 cup heavy whipping cream

This shortcake, handed down through Tom's family for generations, started with his great-grandmother Becky Blake, from Abilene. In her day, people grew their own fragile little berries that never would have made it to a supermarket. These days, strawberries are bred for sturdiness instead of flavor, but by macerating them in sugar and then warming them gently, every bit of sweetness can be coaxed out.

1. To Make the Biscuits: Heat the oven to 450°F. Line a baking sheet with parchment paper or a silicone baking mat.

Stir together the flour, sugar, baking powder, baking soda, and salt in a large shallow bowl. Cut in the butter with the back of large fork, incorporating it until pea-size. Pour in the buttermilk and, using your hands, mix with a minimum of strokes into a smooth dough. Lightly flour a work surface, transfer the dough to it, and roll out to a generous ½-inch thickness. Using a floured 3-inch biscuit cutter, cut the dough into rounds. Between cutting out the biscuits, dip the cutter into some flour so the dough doesn't stick. Lightly pat together any remaining dough scraps, reroll gently, and cut into rounds. Transfer the biscuits to a baking sheet. Brush the biscuit tops lightly with the melted butter, then sprinkle with sugar. Bake, rotating the pan after 10 minutes, for 18 to 20 minutes total, until the biscuits are raised and golden brown.

2. To Prepare the Strawberries: Meanwhile, combine the strawberries with the sugar in a medium saucepan. Let sit for 15 minutes for the juices to come to the surface. Warm over medium heat until the juices begin to thicken.

3. To Serve: Halve the biscuits and arrange each bottom on a dessert plate. Using half of the strawberries, spoon equal amounts over the biscuit bottoms. Place the top half of each biscuit over the berries, then spoon the remaining berries equally over the biscuit tops. Serve right away with cream poured over and around each portion.

Jalapeño Cheesecake

SERVES 12 OR MORE

CRUST

¾ cup graham cracker crumbs

¾ cup chopped pecans

¼ cup granulated sugar

¼ cup (½ stick) salted butter, at room temperature

FILLING

1 jalapeño, quartered and seeded

Three 8-ounce packages (1½ pounds) cream cheese

½ cup granulated sugar

1 tablespoon fresh lemon juice

1 teaspoon pure vanilla extract

3 large eggs

TOPPING

8 ounces sour cream

1 tablespoon granulated sugar

1 tablespoon fresh lemon juice

Jalapeño jelly, for serving

1 whole pickled jalapeño per slice, optional

Along with our bread pudding, this cheesecake is our most popular dessert at the Steakhouse. The combination of heat and sweet surprises many diners. When they have trouble imagining it, we often mention the favorite Texas appetizer of pepper jelly on cream cheese, and the light bulb goes on. We top each slice, before it heads to a table, with a whole pickled jalapeño. Feel free to do the same if you have a flair for the dramatic.

1. Heat the oven to 350°F.

2. **To Make the Crust:** Combine the graham cracker crumbs, pecans, and sugar in a food processor. Pulse in rapid bursts until the mixture is smooth. Add the butter and pulse until the butter is absorbed. Pour the crumb mixture into a 10-inch springform pan. Using your fingers or the back of a spoon, firmly press the crust smoothly on the bottom and about 1 inch up the sides of the pan. Bake the crust for 10 minutes. Remove from the oven and let cool for 5 minutes.

3. **To Make the Filling:** Pulse the jalapeño in the food processor to mince. Add the cream cheese, sugar, lemon juice, and vanilla and blend until smooth. Add the eggs and mix again until combined. Pour the filling into the crust. Using a spatula, smooth the top. Bake the cheesecake for 1 hour, until the center is just set.

4. **To Make the Topping:** While the cheesecake is baking, whisk together the sour cream, sugar, and lemon juice in a small bowl.

5. When the cheesecake is done, remove from the oven and evenly spread on the topping. Return the cheesecake to the oven for an additional 10 minutes, or until the topping has set. Cool completely on a wire baking rack. Cover and refrigerate for at least 3 hours, or up to overnight.

6. To serve, slice the cake with a knife that has been dipped in hot water. Spoon 1 to 2 tablespoons jalapeño jelly over each slice before serving.

A CAKE OF CHEESES

One of our most remarked-upon presentations for a wedding was not a conventional cake, or even a cheesecake, per se, but a cake of cheese. At the request of the bride and groom, we put together a six-layer extravaganza with side garnishes of Italian *salume*. The round cheeses were set on top of each other in decreasing size, just like a tiered wedding cake. At the bottom was a nutty rosemary Asiago followed by a six-month aged Piave. Next came a classic Basque sheep's milk Ossau Iraty AOC followed by a Brie Couronne coated with cracked black pepper. Another Brie, a slightly milder, sweeter Martin-Collet Petit Brie, came next. Topping it all was a Chaource with the aroma of mushrooms and cream. The accompanying cured meats included beef bresaola, pork sopressa Veneta, *finocchiona* (fennel-infused) *salume*, and a smoky speck, or ham, from the southern Alps.

Mexican Wedding Cookies

MAKES ABOUT 4 DOZEN

2 cups all-purpose flour

½ teaspoon table salt

½ teaspoon ground cinnamon

¼ teaspoon ground cloves

¼ teaspoon ground cardamom, optional

1 cup (2 sticks) unsalted butter, softened

⅓ cup granulated sugar

1 teaspoon pure vanilla extract

2 teaspoons water

1 cup chopped pecans, toasted in a dry skillet

1 cup confectioners' sugar, sifted

Some folks know these as Russian tea cakes, but around Texas, they're called Mexican wedding cookies. We add a bit of spice to the dough, as well as the signature pecans and powdered sugar. Bet you can't eat just one.

1. Heat the oven to 350°F. Line 2 baking sheets with parchment paper or silicone baking mats.

2. In a mixing bowl, stir together the flour, salt, cinnamon, cloves, and cardamom (if using). Set aside.

3. With an electric mixer on high speed, beat together the butter and sugar for several minutes until light and fluffy, then add the vanilla and water, and continue beating until incorporated. On low speed, add about half of the flour mixture, then add the rest as the first flour disappears into the mixture. Beat just until the flour is blended, stopping if needed to scrape down the bowl. By hand, mix in the pecans.

4. Roll into 1-inch balls. Place on baking sheets, leaving 1½ to 2 inches between the cookies.

5. Bake for 15 to 18 minutes, until smelling nutty and just set. They should not be brown. At the halfway point, exchange the position of the sheets on the racks from top to bottom and from front to back. Cool the cookies on the baking sheets for 5 minutes, then, while still warm, roll in the confectioners' sugar. Transfer to baking racks to cool completely.

Salted Cinnamon Cookies

MAKES ABOUT 4 DOZEN

TOPPING

1 teaspoon cinnamon

¼ cup granulated sugar

3 cups all-purpose flour

2 teaspoons cream of tartar

1 teaspoon baking soda

2½ teaspoons cinnamon

½ teaspoon fine sea salt

1 cup (2 sticks) unsalted butter

1⅓ cups granulated sugar

1 large egg

2 teaspoons pure vanilla extract

3 tablespoons coarse sea salt or kosher salt

We find these a perfect afternoon pick-me-up. Sweet, but balanced by the nice hit of sea salt and cinnamon.

1. Heat the oven to 375°F. Line 2 baking sheets with parchment paper or silicone baking mats.

2. Combine the cinnamon and sugar in a small bowl. Set aside.

3. In a mixing bowl, stir together the flour, cream of tartar, baking soda, cinnamon, and fine sea salt. Set aside.

4. Using an electric mixer with the paddle attachment, cream the butter on medium speed for 1 minute. Add the sugar and continue beating until fluffy and light in color, another minute or 2. Stop the mixer, scrape down the sides, and add the egg and vanilla. Beat again on medium until combined. Reduce the speed to low and mix in the dry mixture, adding it in three increments. Stop to scrape down the sides of the bowl as needed. The dough will be very thick.

5. Form the dough into tablespoon-size balls, then roll in the cinnamon-sugar mixture. Place on baking sheets, leaving 1½ to 2 inches between the cookies. Sprinkle each with some of the coarse sea salt.

6. Bake for 10 to 12 minutes, until just lightly browned and set. At the halfway point, exchange the position of the sheets on the racks from top to bottom and from front to back. Cool the cookies on the baking sheets for 1 to 2 minutes, then remove them to baking racks to cool completely.

Kahlúa Brownies

MAKES ABOUT 2 DOZEN

Butter

One 18.3- to 18.5-ounce package brownie mix, such as Pillsbury Chocolate Fudge Brownie Mix

1 large egg, beaten

½ cup Kahlúa or other coffee liqueur

¼ cup vegetable oil

¾ cup milk chocolate chips

½ cup semisweet chocolate chips

½ cup chopped pecans, toasted

Confectioners' sugar, optional

Everyone loves a brownie. You can make a boxed mix taste extra special by adding a generous pour of coffee liqueur to it.

1. Heat the oven to 350°F. Butter a 9 x 13-inch baking pan.

2. In a mixing bowl, stir together the brownie mix, egg, Kahlúa, and oil and mix just until combined. Don't overmix. Stir in both chocolate chips and the pecans.

3. Spread the batter (which will be thick) in the prepared pan, smoothing the surface. Bake for 25 to 28 minutes, until the top looks lightly set and a toothpick inserted into the center comes out almost, but not quite clean. Avoid overcooking the brownies—when they look completely done, they'll be too dry.

4. Cool the brownies in the pan. Cut to your preferred size. We make squares of about 2 inches. Slicing is easiest if you wipe the knife blade after each cut. Shortly before serving, if you wish, dust the brownies with confectioners' sugar, sifted through a fine-mesh sieve.

Ginger Blondies

MAKES ABOUT 2 DOZEN

2 cups all-purpose flour

1 tablespoon ground ginger

1½ teaspoons ground cinnamon

1 teaspoon baking powder

¼ teaspoon ground nutmeg

¾ cup plus 2 tablespoons unsalted butter, at room temperature, plus more for pan

1¼ cups granulated sugar

3 tablespoons molasses

2 tablespoons light corn syrup

2 large eggs

¼ cup chopped crystallized ginger

Confectioners' sugar

Here's a deliciously chewy alternative to the more expected chocolate-rich brownies. The double dose of ginger is irresistible.

1. Heat the oven to 350°F. Butter a 9X13-inch baking pan.

2. Stir together the flour, ground ginger, cinnamon, baking powder, and nutmeg.

3. With an electric mixer on high speed, beat together the butter and sugar for several minutes until light and fluffy, then add the molasses and corn syrup and continue beating on medium speed until well incorporated. Mix in the eggs one at a time, beating until each is blended. On low speed, add about half of the flour mixture, then add the rest as the first flour disappears into the mixture. Beat just until the flour is blended, stopping if needed to scrape down the sides of the bowl. Stir in the crystallized ginger by hand.

4. Spread the batter (which will be thick) in the prepared pan, smoothing the surface. Bake for 22 to 25 minutes, until the top looks just set and a toothpick inserted into the center comes out almost, but not quite clean. Avoid overcooking the blondies—when they look completely done, they'll be too dry.

5. Cool the blondies in the pan. Cut to your preferred size. We make squares of about 2 inches and then bisect them into triangles. Slicing is easiest if you wipe the knife blade after each cut. Shortly before serving, dust the blondies with confectioners' sugar, sifted through a fine-mesh sieve.

TEXAS-SIZE SPREADS FOR YOUR CELEBRATIONS

We truly believe that good things happen at the dinner table. You might remember that it was catering that kicked off our Steakhouse business. Oh my, how it's grown from those early days, when Tom hauled his chuck wagon to other ranches to supply the food and a good helping of cowboy ambiance for cattle auctions, horse sales, and other events in our general vicinity. Over some four decades, that original wagon has traveled overseas, to both coasts, and even to the White House. Tom designed the horse trailer it travels in, and once it rolls out, the trailer transforms into a mobile kitchen. We can create all kinds of celebratory meals out of that trailer. These days we find ourselves at every kind of event, from bull sales to elaborate ranch weddings. We've substantially expanded our repertoire to accommodate everything from morning brunches to late night noshes. See our French-Fried French Toast, page 42, for a dish that works on both of those ends of the spectrum, and doesn't cost a lot either. No matter if big or small, grand or rustic, the characteristic that ties all of these events and spreads of food together is the bounty, the sense of generosity we work to achieve for our catering clients as well as our Steakhouse guests.

Catering and events are always full of curve-balls, and no matter how much experience you have, it seems like there's often a surprise. Our team is really good at overcoming these small challenges. We didn't always know what we were doing. We have learned that not all ovens are equal, and our pans don't fit in most, so now

we bring our own ovens. One time, our truck wouldn't fit under a gate to enter an event, so we had to let some of the air out of our tires and creep under the gate.

To host a memorable event, don't feel like entertaining requires that classic chuck wagon, a perfectly set table, or multiple sit-down courses. It certainly shouldn't require stressing out for days in advance. A simple weeknight supper of a fun tailgate spread can be a very memorable celebration. We hope that we can inspire you with some of these ideas and recipes, and with goods from our store, Perini Ranch Country Market (some available online at periniranch.com).

What you choose to serve and how you present it should reflect who you are. Here we give you a passel of possibilities for your own gatherings, but as the kids say today, "You do you." It's not necessary to create every dish suggested. Maybe pick one for the centerpiece, and serve it with a salad. Maybe start with something like our Smoked Salmon Potato Chips (page 80), which are super simple but make people feel special.

Beyond these suggestions of dishes for various occasions, our single best piece of advice comes from Lisa. She says "I live for lists. Always make a list. Make multiple lists. Put every detail down, as you think of it." On any given day, you may not get through the whole list, but you'll feel substantial accomplishments as you see numerous items crossed off. For any event, think of how many steps you can do in advance, so that you can enjoy your own party. If you're enjoying yourself, your guests will too.

ENTERTAINING TIPS

Figure out if you want to serve casually with a buffet, or family style at the table. More formally would be to arrange each plate by course, and remember this takes more hands in the kitchen. We think there's a time and place for all these styles of service. For a buffet, we've been known to give folks baking sheets to load up with all their favorites. That always brings a smile.

Maybe serve the main dish and sides at the table, but have an appetizer bar or a dessert bar for people to help themselves. A s'mores bar remains a perennial favorite for all ages. We've found that your guests really like to move around and mingle.

For the pre-dinner nibbles, pick items that can be devoured as finger foods. Avoiding plates and utensils is key—keep those hands free for your cocktail! If you have no time to make appetizers, just put together a selection of cheeses, cool-looking crackers, and some jams or other condiments on a wooden board.

Can the rest of the meal go on one plate, or is it going to require a separate salad plate? Visualizing how the food will look on the plate is important. You want a variety of colors, shapes, and textures to make a pretty plate presentation. The old saying is true—you eat first with your eyes.

Table décor can be as simple or elaborate as you want to make it. At the Steakhouse, we have mismatched wooden tables and chairs, and we like the feel of wood, with no need for linens. However, for events, we often use linens as a part of the décor, but our style is best suited to a beautiful wood table.

Your tableware doesn't have to match or be expensive. Melamine and spattered enamel-covered metal work great for the kinds of dishes in this book. Cast-iron pots and griddles can be used for cooking of course, but they also look rustically great for serving on a buffet. Galvanized tubs and buckets of various sizes and shapes can hold ice and drinks. They're inexpensive at feed and farm supply stores. Look for serving pieces, glassware, wooden boards, and flatware at estate sales or resale and thrift shops. We are huge collectors of serving pieces, tabletop items, and things that enhance the dining experience. At home, we love to set the table and almost always light our candles. It feels like a celebration, even when having leftovers. For our events, our buffets are typically a combination of antique wooden bowls, sterling silver, copper, and cast iron. Somehow, all that can work together.

There's no reason that a spread has to be an evening event. We give you a few options here for daytime entertaining. Weekend breakfast can be unexpected fun. Add a cocktail if you want, but you can also get by with coffee and a fruit juice blend.

Do you have enough seating for the number of people you're inviting? You may not need a seat for everyone simultaneously if it's patio cocktails, although even then it's helpful, especially if your guests are older. If the event is outdoors, maybe bring out some of your indoor furniture. You might pick up inexpensive bales of straw and throw some Mexican blankets over them. If it happens to be an outdoor evening event, do you have enough lighting?

We encourage you to gather your folks together soon. Use these suggested spreads as a guide to create your own Texas-spirited event.

The Really Big Signature Perini Ranch Spread

Our classics, with a little something for everyone. This has become our Signature Menu and for those that are new to Perini Ranch, sometimes they are a little surprised with the pairing of Mesquite Smoked Peppered Beef Tenderloin and Southern Fried Catfish, but these are the two stars of our show!

Back to Brisket

We aren't officially a barbecue joint, but we are a joint, with a couple of really fine barbecue classics. Initially, Tom served more smoked brisket than grilled steaks. We still offer brisket as a special and always have it available by mail order. Ribs are a staple here, featured on our dinner menu nightly. Serve these two meats with a couple of our most popular sides, ones that go back to Tom's early catering days.

SPECIAL STEAK DINNER

Special Steak Dinner

Not much compares with a great ribeye, no matter what you might be celebrating. Add in a selection from these vegetables, and finish with cheesecake that adds a little kick.

Cowboy Ribeye Steaks, page 138

Spicy Brussels Sprouts, page 210

Bourbon-Glazed Carrots, page 213

Cowboy Potatoes, page 221

Grilled Sourdough Slices with Green Onion Butter, page 246

Jalapeño Cheesecake, page 276

Sunday Lunch

For many years, we've offered a Sunday buffet featuring these glories of Texas fried foods—chicken and chicken-fried—steak that is. The meal always requires a reservation, as we cook to order. If you only want to tackle one of the main dishes at home, we know your guests will still be ecstatic. Our Sunday lunch has become a staple of spring holidays. For Easter and Mothers' Day, we might serve over 700 guests. We're so honored to see families gather with us year after year.

The Judge's Fried Chicken, 180

Chicken-Fried Steak with Cream Gravy, page 160

Mashed Potatoes, page 222

Texas Chocolate Sheet Cake, page 258

Chuck Wagon Breakfast

Oh my, this makes a fine way to start a special day. Out on the range, the classic biscuits would have been sourdough, made in a Dutch oven with coals shoveled over the top. Even a serious cowboy cook like Tom appreciates that you can whip these up now with baking powder and pop them right in the oven. The casserole can go in the oven too while you finish up the gravy and hash browns. And, of course, all meals eaten outside taste better!

Fish Fry

Every summer from Easter through Labor Day, we offer an outdoor fish fry. Southern fried catfish, golden jalapeño hushpuppies, homemade tartar and cocktail sauces, and grilled lemons. Cowboys (and cowgirls) love catfish. Go figure...

Easter Dinner

Our most memorable Easter meal was during the pandemic, when we served more than 200 to-go dinners, drive-up style. What an operation! It looked like the Dallas Cowboys stadium on game day. Celebrate the coming of spring with some or all of these luscious choices.

Deviled eggs

Smoked ham from your favorite source

Tom's Italian Big Night

Abbondanza! These are a few favorites from the Perini *famiglia*. We're so proud of our Swiss Italian heritage, and it's fun to cook like we're in Italy!

Small Town 4th of July Picnic

Hot dogs and burgers on the grill, with all the fixings

Ham biscuits (thin-sliced country ham with mustard and chutney on our Buttermilk Biscuits on page 240)

Country Potato Salad, page 110

Roasted Corn on the Cob, page 217

Peach-Bourbon Cobbler, page 272, with vanilla ice cream

Sliced watermelon

Sweet tea and/or cold beer

What's more fun than fireworks and festivities celebrating the birth of our nation? It's usually sultry enough for hens to lay hard-boiled eggs, but that doesn't stop folks from gathering around the grill for burgers, dogs, and more.

Patio Cocktails, Southwest Style

We love al fresco dining, and in nice weather you'll always find us outside at cocktail hour, either at home or at the Steakhouse. Foods from Mexico and New Mexico have heavily influenced our cooking, and we love this menu. Whether it's Tuesday or any other day of the week, tacos are always welcome. Make sure you have enough small plates and napkins to go along with them though. Make up a pitcher of margaritas and that West Texas classic, ranch water, a slightly lighter tequila drink. Round out with pecan-coated bacon and that all-around favorite, guacamole.

Board "Meating"

The Ranch Salad, page 100

Strip Steaks, page 142

Beef Filets with Blue Cheese Butter, page 145

Grilled Spinalis Dorsi, page 139, or Cowboy Ribeye Steaks, page 138

Pecan Bars, page 266

For dedicated carnivores, a mixed grill of several kinds of steaks can be the ultimate pleasure. We add to a couple of regular menu items a very special cut called spinalis dorsi, or ribeye cap. It's not always available from a butcher, but worth its premium price when you can find it.

Cowboy Charcuterie

You have to think a bit ahead, but for an important party, you can order a selection of our beef mail-order items from periniranch.com, and supplement them with a few store-bought condiments. We make the beef sticks from tenderloins, and the sausage is 100% beef brisket.

Mesquite Smoked Peppered Beef Tenderloin

Beef Sticks

Mesquite Smoked Beef Sausage with Green Chile

Olives, cheeses, and pickles

Grilled breads or crackers

Dove Hunt

Dove hunting season, which opens September 1, is a big deal in Texas. You don't find dove available commercially but if you or a friend hunts, the breasts are the part of the bird that is prized. They can dry out easily, so often get the wrapped-in-bacon treatment. We season with ours first with a little of our citrus-and-rosemary Fish & Fowl Rub, but salt and pepper works just fine too. We grill the breasts for the assembled hunters and friends, over medium heat, and move them around the cooking grate as needed to avoid flare-ups from the bacon. We also grill up steaks for those who have worked up a bigger appetite.

Dove breasts, wrapped in bacon and grilled

Strip Steaks, page 142

Corn and Shishito Salad, page 103

Banana Pudding, page 261, served in half-pint Mason jars with their screw-on metal rims

Football Tailgate

Whether the football's at high school, college, or pro level, and whether you're actually in the lot or watching on TV, a hearty and festive tailgate-style spread makes a win sweeter and a loss easier to swallow.

Texas Chili, page 163

Frito pies (Pour chili over Fritos and top with chopped tomatoes and onion, and grated Cheddar. This is particularly sporty served in individual-size Frito packages, slit down the side.)

Lowcountry boil of shrimp, corn on the cob, onions, and potatoes

Ham and Hawaiian roll sandwiches (Slice a bag of Hawaiian rolls horizontally, brush with melted butter flavored with Dijon mustard, Worcestershire sauce, and poppy seeds, then top with layers of thin-sliced ham and Swiss cheese. Brush tops with more butter, wrap in foil, and bake about 15 minutes at 350°F until oozy.)

Ginger Blondies, page 283, Pecan Bars, page 266, and Apple Pie Bars, page 270

Shiner Bock, Lone Star, and a selection of other beers

Thanksgiving Spread

Tom roasts the turkeys around here. He gives them a light coat of our rosemary-and-citrus-scented Fish & Fowl Rub under and over the skin, then lets the bird soak up the flavor over night before oven roasting. It's a tradition that daughter Jessica makes the gravy, as her gravy just can't be beaten. Some people tell us, at least jokingly, that they serve our brown sugar–enriched sweet potatoes as dessert. We, however, figure it's a fine day to offer them on the side and indulge in a couple of final flourishes—a pie and a crisp. It's a time for celebrating family and giving thanks for our abundant blessings.

Christmas Eve Pit Party

By the time we've shipped out some thousands of mesquite-smoked peppered beef tenderloins between Thanksgiving and Christmas, even we take off a night from meat. The Steakhouse is slammed on this evening, so we build a blazing wood fire out back to take the chill off the winter's night. We gather 'round the fire with a few friends and staff for a simple seafood feast, warming a pot of gumbo and grilling oysters to slurp down. After the harried finish to mail-order season and the numerous holiday parties hosted at the restaurant and in our Supper Club, it's a fun way to come together and enjoy the real spirit of the season.

Char-grilled oysters on the half-shell

Shrimp and Sausage Gumbo, page 189

Traditional Holiday Spread

On Christmas Day, we alternate between the classic dinner of roasted prime rib here, and the following less formal Southwestern spread.

Cocktails and mocktails with crushed peppermint rims

Ranch Roasted Prime Rib, page 152

Yorkshire puddings made with beef tallow

Southern Sweet Potatoes with Brown Sugar Pecans, page 230

Spicy Brussels Sprouts, page 210

Pear-Cranberry Crisp, page 262

Good Cabernet Sauvignon, such as those from Becker Vineyards

Feliz Navidad

The prime rib spread above is always a Christmas Day hit, but for variety's sake, we mix it up with this more casual Southwestern spread. We think you and your family and friends will love either.

Local tamales

Beef Fajitas, page 165

Carne Guisada, page 164

Pico de Gallo, page 60

Black Bean and Roasted Corn Salad, page 105

Tres Leches Cake, page 260

Mexican Wedding Cookies, page 278

Mesquite-a-Rita, page 86

Ring in the New Year
in Boots and Jeans

Smoked Salmon Potato Chips,
page 80

A decadent cheese board

A tin of caviar served with Pringles
potato chips and crème fraîche

Champagne, the best you can afford

When you're in the hospitality business, you work really hard during the holidays, and so we love New Year's Eve at home, sometimes with a handful of close friends, and of course our herd of hound dogs. Dressed down, we have a fire in our living room and indulge in this simple but luscious combo. We need little more than each other and those friends to toast to our gratitude about living our dream, home on the ranch.

Acknowledgments

The most important thing that Tom and I can tell you about our business and our projects is that we understand that our team is our biggest asset. Nothing is possible here at the ranch without the commitment and dedication of each and every person that works here. With that said, the same holds true for this book—it has been a labor of love by many. From the Perini Ranch crew—special thanks to long time managers and cooks Dale Cronk, Jason Mayes, John Montgomery, and Jo-Anna Jackson, who worked together to create almost every recipe for photography and answered one million questions about each recipe.

Our co-author, Cheryl Alters Jamison, has worked with us on several projects over the years. She and her late husband, Bill, became dear friends after a chance encounter through a mutual friend. Since Cheryl has four James Beard Foundation Awards for cookbooks hanging in her kitchen, we decided to hitch ourselves to Cheryl and have her help tell our story. She also tested each and every recipe for accuracy. All of her work has been such a contribution to this project.

Another long-time friend, Wyatt McSpadden, and his assistant Rick Patrick, can make everything look good through the lens of Wyatt's camera. In the restaurant business, it's always front-of-mind that people eat with their eyes first, so food has to look good before it tastes good. Wyatt makes that happen with every photograph. We also love it that he says he "makes" photographs, not "takes" photographs! A few photos are from our archives and are the work of several other great photographers—Michele Sparks, Logan Dyer, and others. Michele is an integral part of our team, managing social media, photography, and marketing projects.

And, making a good photo also involves setting the stage so that the photography tells the story and relays the sense of place. Our new friend, food stylist Tina Bell Stamos, is a true gift to this project. Not only has she been patient with us, but she has embraced the Perini Ranch style and has taught us how to look even better! Tina worked closely on this project with our Catering and Events Manager, Suzanne Travis. Suzanne jokingly refers to herself as the "parts department" here at the ranch, and she's vital to the success of each and every Perini Ranch catering and event.

Thanks as well to our new friends at Cider Mill Press and HarperCollins. You never know what opportunities might come your way, and where things might lead. Suzanne and I had a chance encounter with Cider Mill Press founder and publisher, John Whalen, while we were on a buying trip in Atlanta for our Country Market. We had a fun conversation about the ranch and our previous books, exchanged numbers, and went on our way. Soon after, John just happened to "pass through" Buffalo Gap on a cross-country road trip. And suddenly, here we were, with an unexpected opportunity to publish our recipes and stories, and share them with a new audience.

Tom and I have come to realize that a lot of business success is a result of unexpected opportunities. When these happen, you make a decision—to either participate or just talk about it. We have had so many examples of this in our decades together. Every time we have chosen to jump in, we've been terrifically pleased with the results.

Again, thanks to each and every member of the Perini Ranch family. We appreciate you more than you know.

—Lisa

CONVERSION TABLE

WEIGHTS

1 oz. = 28 grams
2 oz. = 57 grams
4 oz. (¼ lb.) = 113 grams
8 oz. (½ lb.) = 227 grams
16 oz. (1 lb.) = 454 grams

VOLUME MEASURES

⅛ teaspoon = 0.6 ml
¼ teaspoon = 1.23 ml
½ teaspoon = 2.5 ml
1 teaspoon = 5 ml
1 tablespoon (3 teaspoons) = ½ fluid oz. = 15 ml
2 tablespoons = 1 fluid oz. = 29.5 ml
¼ cup (4 tablespoons) = 2 fluid oz. = 59 ml
⅓ cup (5⅓ tablespoons) = 2.7 fluid oz. = 80 ml
½ cup (8 tablespoons) = 4 fluid oz. = 120 ml
⅔ cup (10⅔ tablespoons) = 5.4 fluid oz. = 160 ml
¾ cup (12 tablespoons) = 6 fluid oz. = 180 ml
1 cup (16 tablespoons) = 8 fluid oz. = 240 ml

TEMPERATURE EQUIVALENTS

°F	°C	Gas Mark
225	110	¼
250	130	½
275	140	1
300	150	2
325	170	3
350	180	4
375	190	5
400	200	6
425	220	7
450	230	8
475	240	9
500	250	10

LENGTH MEASURES

1/16 inch = 1.6 mm
⅛ inch = 3 mm
¼ inch = 6.35 mm
½ inch = 1.25 cm
¾ inch = 2 cm
1 inch = 2.5 cm

INDEX

About Cider Mill Press
Book Publishers

Good ideas ripen with time. From seed to harvest, Cider Mill Press brings fine reading, information, and entertainment together between the covers of its creatively crafted books. Our Cider Mill bears fruit twice a year, publishing a new crop of titles each spring and fall.

"Where Good Books Are Ready for Press"

501 Nelson Place
Nashville, Tennessee 37214

cidermillpress.com